GOOD FOOD, MILK FREE, GRAIN FREE

Keats Publishing Titles of Relevant Interest

The Additives Book—Beatrice Trum Hunter

The Do It Yourself Allergy Analysis Handbook—Kate Ludeman, Ph.D., and Louise Henderson

Good Food, Gluten Free—Hilda Cherry Hills

Good Foods That Go Together—Elinor L. Smith

Mental and Elemental Nutrients—Carl C. Pfeiffer, Ph.D., M.D.

Recipe for Survival—Doris Grant

Your Body Is Your Best Doctor—Melvin E. Page, D.D.S., and H. Leon Abrams, Jr., Ph.D.

GOOD FOOD, MILK FREE, GRAIN FREE

Hilda Cherry Hills

Introduction by Beatrice Trum Hunter

Keats Publishing, Inc. New Canaan, Connecticut

Royalties from the "Good Food" series all go to the Henry Doubleday Research Association of Convent Lane, Bocking, Braintree, Essex, England, an international charity working on gardening and farming without chemicals for the people of all countries (founder and director, Lawrence D. Hills). Mrs. Hilda Cherry Hills will be happy to reply to any queries concerning her books sent to the above address with an International Coupon to ensure return postage and a self-addressed envelope.

GOOD FOOD, MILK FREE, GRAIN FREE

Health Science Edition published in 1980 by
Keats Publishing, Inc. By arrangement with
Roberts Publications, London, England

Library of Congress Catalog Card Number: 79-87834

ISBN: 0-87983-200-2 (Clothbound)
0-87983-201-0 (Paperback)

Printed in the United States of America

Keats Publishing, Inc.
27 Pine Street (Box 876)
New Canaan, Connecticut 06840

DEDICATED TO

Anyone, anywhere, at any time, who cares about and works at helping the mentally ill.

CONTENTS

Foreword to the American Edition

It is possible to avoid milk, grains, and other common allergens provided one eats simply and chooses foods in their primary state. However, with current American food and beverage processing techniques developed in increasingly sophisticated ways, it has become virtually impossible to detect the presence of these possible allergens that certain individuals need to avoid. To have a thorough knowledge, one would need to become an expert in the field of food science and technology.

Corn serves as an excellent example. Those who must avoid corn or corn fractions, may encounter it in at least 150 unanticipated ways.

When sugar prices soared in the mid 1970s, many food and beverage processors switched from cane sugar to the use of high-fructose corn syrup and other corn-based sweeteners for their products. Hence, although canned fruits must have "sugar added" on the label of sweetened products, the consumer has no way of knowing if the added sugar consists wholely or partly of corn sugar in some form. Similarly, canned and frozen peas, beans and carrots may also contain added sugars of unspecified origins.

Although a food product may list "molasses" on the label, what remains unstated is that the sweetener may be made from a spray-dried, free-flowing molasses concentrate that contains corn syrup solids as a flow agent.

A dry powdered lemon juice, used by processors in food manufacture, is mixed with corn syrup. The final processed food, sold at the retail level, merely states "lemon juice" in the ingredient listing. The corn syrup is present as a hidden offender for the person who needs to avoid corn.

A new addition to a line of cake-depanning compounds consists in part of cornstarch, designed for efficient release of many bakery goods.

Dehydrated fruit products, available to the baking industry, contain modified food starch, which can be made from corn or other grains. Dehydrated fruits and vegetable flakes and granules, including beet, carrot, apple, pear, peach, apricot and lemon, are treated with modified food starch, and then used for fruit juices, sauces, gravies, soups, dips, spreads, jellies and jams. Modified food starch may also replace as much as a third of the fruit solids in products such as commercial applesauce; and as much as half of the coconut in confections. Bakers can cut egg costs in half by using a mixture that includes corn syrup in the ingredients.

Peanut butter, a popular American foodstuff, commonly contains added sugar. Frequently, the sugar is corn-based.

Most baking powders contain cornstarch. Some leavening yeasts also contain cornstarch, although corn-free dry yeast is available.

"Sugar cured" bacons and ham contain corn sugar (glucose or dextrose).

Many brands of iodized table salt contain dextrose to help stabilize the iodine compound.

Most acetic acid vinegars used commercially are manufactured from corn.

Corn oil is used commonly in prepared salad dressings, deep fat frying, and in processing potato chips. With many processed foods, it is impossible to know, from label reading, if corn oil is contained in "vegetable oil." Even if one chooses another vegetable oil, specifically labeled, it may be contaminated with corn oil. Edible vegetable oils are transported in bulk, and the tank shipment may vary from one oil to another, on different occasions.

Corn-derived alcohol is commonly used as a component in food flavoring extracts such as vanilla, lemon and almond.

Since the price of coffee has risen, corn-based coffee replacers are used to extend ground coffee. Many instant coffees contain corn sugar (dextrose or glucose).

Domestically processed alcoholic beverages often contain added sugar, which may be corn-based. An exception is California wine, with an alcohol content up to 13 percent;

fortified wines, with an alcoholic content over 13 percent, as well as domestically produced brandies may, and usually do contain added corn sugar. All whiskey, vodka, gin, ale and beer are corn products. Blended Scotch, prepared in Scotland for American export, is excessively "bourbonized" (corn-containing). Nine out of ten American breweries are reported to use corn grits or corn flakes as a cereal adjunct to produce beer more economically.

An examination of other grains, as they appear in modern food and beverage processing, demonstrates similar problems as corn and corn fractions. Wheat, for example, appears in unexpected places, as a replacer ingredient. By way of illustration, General Foods' "Mellow Roast," has wheat combined with coffee beans in the ground product; and wheat, molasses and bran in the instant product.

Milk fractions are also difficult to avoid in processed foods and beverages, since they, too, appear in unlikely places. Dairy Research, Inc. has reported extensively about technological advances having generated new methods for processing milk to provide greater opportunities to use dairy-based ingredients in processed foods such as meat products and meat-substitute products; gravies and soups; vegetables and fruit products; beverages; cereals and pasta products; and snack foods.

Lactose, or milk sugar, has many uses by processors of meat, candy, baked goods and baby foods. It is also used as a carrier for food flavors.

Nonfat milk powder is frequently used as a binder in sausages.

Even so-called nondairy products may contain milk fractions, such as sodium caseinate, which is a milk protein. For some illogical reason, the Food and Drug Administration classifies sodium caseinate as a chemical additive, and hence "nondairy" products may actually contain a dairy product.

One milk fraction, lactic acid, which develops in cultured milk products, is extensively used by food processors, yet may not appear on food labels. Among other food items, lactic acid is used with bakery products, beer, beverages, bologna, candies, cervelat, cheese products, confections, cottage cheese, dried egg white, dry sausages, gelatine desserts, frozen desserts, fruit jellies and jams, ices, Lebanon bologna, olives, pickles, pork rolls, puddings, sherbets and toppings. Also, lactylic esters of fatty acids are prepared from lactic acid combined with fatty acids, and used as emulsifiers, plasticizers and surfactants with shortenings and edible fats and oils used with bakery mixes, baked products, cake icings, fillings and toppings; dehydrated fruits and vegetables as well as their juices; frozen desserts; liquid shortenings; pancake mixes; precooked instant rice; pudding mixes; solid-state edible emulsions consisting of fat and water, and used in non-dairy creamers. *It is obvious that one needs to avoid all factory-processed fabricated food in order to avoid hidden milk fractions.*

In addition to being aware of the presence of grain and milk fractions in unlikely places in foods and beverages, alertness is important with other consumer goods. For example, it is necessary to know the exact composition of food supplements. Most tablets or pills, and capsules, contain cornstarch as excipients, binders or fillers. Synthetic vitamin C is manufactured from glucose, a corn sugar. Milk sugar is also used in supplements.

Toiletries and pharmaceutical products may contain corn fractions. Bath and body talcum powders may contain cornstarch, and induce adverse reactions if inhaled. (Similarly, the fumes from corn being cooked, or from clothing being ironed, which has been treated with cornstarch to stiffen the fabric, may induce reactions in individuals sensitive to corn.) Dentifrices, aspirin, suppositories and excipients or diluents in lozenges or ointments may contain corn fractions.

Many consumer items also contain corn. These include adhesives used in gums to make postage stamps, sticker tapes and sealing gums on envelopes. Some paper packaging used with food contains corn. Paper cups, plates and boxes containing moist food, may release corn fractions if the packaging is corn-treated. The inner surface of some food wraps may be coated with cornstarch.

Obviously, it is difficult to avoid exposures to food components that may induce adverse reactions in highly susceptible individuals. To a limited degree, careful label reading will help. But it should be apparent that label reading is only the first step. Many exposures will be prevented by choosing foods, insofar as possible, in their primary state, with minimal processing. Any processed foods need to be introduced singly, and in a small quantity, to find out if they are well tolerated. If they are, constant label reading is essential, since food and beverage processors frequently reformulate, with "new" and "improved" products. This practice may affect a susceptible individual in an unanticipated "new" but not "improved" fashion.

Since individuals differ markedly in their tolerance or intolerance for individual foods, there are no easy rules that apply to all. Two simple, but sound principles have evolved. First, the simpler the food preparation, the fewer the problems are apt to occur. And second, the greater the variety within the framework of foods that can be tolerated, the less likelihood there will be of increasing sensitivity to particular foods.

Clinical ecologists have demonstrated the wisdom of these two principles. The most common allergens are those dietary items used most frequently and consistently. Since grains and milk are used both frequently and consistently in our culture, it is little wonder that they are such common allergens. By using primary foods, and rotating them within the diet, many individuals have been able to reduce their sensitivities. (For details, see Theron Randolph's *Human Ecology and Susceptibility to the Chemical Environment*; and Lawrence Dickey, ed., *Clinical Ecology*. Both books were published by Charles Thomas Publishing Company in Springfield, Illinois.)

Beatrice Trum Hunter
Hillsboro, N.H., March, 1980

Foreword to the English Edition

Mrs. Cherry Hills has shown by the great success of her book *Good Food, Gluten Free*, now in its third edition, that there is a need for a comprehensive guide and recipe book for people requiring a special diet.

She has undertaken the compilation of recipes for other elimination diets and this is one of the series, in all of which the principles of good nutrition are promoted.

This one is for a milk-free, grain-free diet which for many years has been shown to be effective in ameliorating symptoms of schizophrenia by Dr. Curtis Dohan of the University of Pennsylvania. His work has recently been corroborated by Dr. Man Mohan Singh as was reported in *Science* in January, 1976.

People are recommended not to abandon any medication they are on, but they may like to discuss with their doctors the possibility of attempting this diet with their treatment. For people with celiac disease a grain-free diet is an extension of the diet they are on—a gluten-free diet. Some celiacs will benefit from this more rigorous exclusion diet. Moreover many celiacs are deficient in lactase, an enzyme present in the intestine which digests the lactose sugar of milk. They cannot take milk or milk products without risking diarrhea, abdominal bloating and wind. Others cannot manage the protein component of milk. It would be wise for celiacs to ask their doctors if they should abstain from milk too.

For people who require such a diet this book will be invaluable and will lead to better health through good nutrition.

PREFACE

This small book marks a stage on the long and arduous road I have followed for over 25 years in an effort to learn all I could about the biochemical approach to the mental illness called schizophrenia. Today this approach offers much hope of control and eventual cure of this distressing disability.

Recently it became clear that I might perhaps add a mite to the outstanding contributions made by the great figures in this field by adapting and compiling recipes which would make the medically recommended exclusion diets acceptable to anyone willing to try them out, and to their families as well.

Indeed, I cherish the hope that those who follow this new way of eating which excludes all grains and all milk products will be rewarded not only by enjoying meals which are palatable, nutritious and varied, but also by finding a noticeable improvement in their response to the medical treatment they are receiving, because they are co-operating by giving up foods which have been found harmful to their condition.

Over the years I have read so many scientific articles, journals and books on mental illness and so many cookery books ranging from Mrs. Beeton to the latest offering in the daily press, that I find it impossible to name the individual writers to whom I am so deeply indebted for the many recipes I have adapted to meet the very special requirements of this diet. I can only apologise for this omission and say, collectively, thank you all the same.

However, I would like to express my gratitude to the following authors and their publishers for permission to quote specific recipes directly. They are Edyth Young Cottrell for an extract on making soya milk from her book "The Oats, Peas, Beans and Barley Cookbook" published in 1974 by the Woodbridge Publishing Company, Santa Barbara, California, and Frieda Nusz for her recipes called "Magic Milk" and "Magic Cream" from her book "The Natural Foods Blender Cookbook" published in 1972 by Keats Publishing Inc., New Canaan, Connecticut. Thanks also to Gladys Harmer for so kindly sending me her recipe for potato flour bread, to Kathleen Gates for testing some recipes and finally to Eunice Farmilant for making many helpful suggestions.

HILDA CHERRY HILLS

Chapter 1

HOW TO FOLLOW A GRAIN-FREE MILK-FREE DIET

Why not try it?

One in five people in Britain today will suffer from some form of mental illness. It is known that certain factors in food can worsen these conditions but that by following a diet from which foods containing the harmful factors are excluded the condition may be alleviated or even cured provided that the diet is rigidly adhered to. These diets in no way interfere with medical treatment. In fact, they can make many drugs more effective although it should be emphasised that it may be some time before the benefits become apparent.

This book is written especially with the needs of people caring for schizophrenia patients in mind. Mothers, wives and others who must cater for such patients often do not realise that the symptoms of intense depression, weariness, apathy, hallucinations and eventual violent feelings of aggression may be relieved by a diet that excludes all milk and milk products and any food obtained from grain or any refined carbohydrates. They would probably feel that such a diet would be inadequate yet millions of healthy and prosperous people in other parts of the world never eat bread. What is more a diet designed for their patients can be no more trouble than cooking for a gourmet and a great deal cheaper.

A recently published report by workers in the United States (Singh, M. M., Kay, S. R., *Science*, 1976, *191*, 401-2) confirms the earlier findings of Dr. F. C. Dohan of Pennsylvania University (*British Journal of Psychiatry*, 1969, *115*, 595-6) that a grain-free diet has a favorable effect on schizophrenia.

Elimination of grain from the diet means that bread, cakes, biscuits or anything else made with flour from wheat, oats, barley, rye, corn, millet or rice must be avoided. Also, it is necessary to avoid constituents such as wheat germ and gluten.

The ban on milk products means that butter, cheese, custards, ice-cream, milk puddings and other milk-containing foods and milk constituents, such as casein, must not be eaten. These two restrictions must be rigidly adhered to. It is not essential to observe so strictly the ban on refined carbohydrates, the most important of which is white sugar, but they are second-rate foods and should be avoided where possible. A number of the recipes do, in fact, include sugar but in each case unrefined or turbinado sugar is specified and that is the form you should use if you wish to use sugar for any other purpose. White sugar and turbinado sugar both contain sucrose. Some mentally ill patients may find that either form disagrees with them and they will of course avoid sugar as strictly as they must avoid milk and grain products.

Surely this is worth trying. It could harm no one. But what to eat and drink? This book contains recipes and guides to what, and what not to eat to help you, if you are a doctor, and your patient to enjoy a diet within the restrictions mentioned.

Meals based on the recommendations and recipes provide foods which are appetizing, palatable, nutritious, inexpensive and versatile, while all are forbidden foods in any form, obvious or hidden are rigidly excluded.

There are also warnings against using (except in strict moderation) certain common foods that are high in calories, but low in minerals and vitamins, and which leave little appetite or room for the more nutritious foods suggested.

Precious digestive juices should not be wasted on second-rate foods.

Your patient, and you, deserve only the best available under the restrictions of a milk-free, grain-free diet. Here is a guide to what the best foods are.

N.B.—If too much weight is lost on the diet the amount of food taken should be increased, especially potatoes and bananas.

YOU MAY EAT

Breakfast at home

Bacon, lean, nitrite-free and *not* sugar-cured	This may be cooked as desired and accompanied by apple, banana, mushroom, potato, potato flour bread (recipe 28) or tomato—baked, boiled, fried, mashed or sautéed (preferable to deep-frying).
Bread	Potato flour bread (recipe 28) plain or toasted.
Condiments	Cloves, cinnamon, nutmeg, paprika, pepper, salt (preferably sea salt because of its good mineral content), spices (if guaranteed grain-free), turmeric powder.
Eggs*	Baked, boiled, coddled, fried, poached or scrambled eggs (use no milk in scrambled eggs) with any of the accompaniments listed under bacon.
Fats	Peanut oil (provided it is guaranteed grain- or gluten-free), olive oil, safflower oil, sesame, soy or sunflower oil. *Be absolutely certain that no corn oil is used.*

*Because of the restrictions imposed by the diet and the ready availability of eggs in restaurants you will probably tend to choose eggs when eating out. Therefore if you eat out regularly restrict your consumption of eggs at home. You should also cut down on eggs if you use much Magic milk or Magic cream, which contain egg.

Fish Any variety, such as mackeral, cod, herring, kippers, roe, sardines (canned in oil but not in sauce), without batter, butter, cheese, crumbs (unless made of potato flour bread), flour (except permitted flours) or sauce. It may be baked, boiled, sautéed, broiled, poached, pickled or steamed and served with any of the accompaniments listed under bacon.

Fruits Any variety of fruit—fresh or canned (water-packed only).

Meats Heart, kidney or liver, which may be baked, boiled, braised (with potato flour), broiled or sautéed and served with any of the accompaniments listed under bacon.

Nuts Any variety. Chestnuts contain no fat. Buy nuts in the shell or without salt or oil. Do not buy "dry-roasted."

Vegetables All varieties, especially dried lentils, peas and beans but excluding sweet corn, canned sweet potatoes, carrots and peas, frozen peas. Lentil, pea, potato and soy flours may be used.

YOU MAY DRINK

Carob This is a cocoa substitute (see beverages p. 14 and recipes 8 and 25).

Coffee Although coffee is undesirable, chicory and dandelion coffee are acceptable. *No* instant coffee. Any of the non-milks may be added. (See pp. 37-41.)

Fruit and vegetable juices Any fresh, or unsweetened bottled or canned, juices. Any vegetable juices.

Milk substitutes Magic milk (recipe 77) or vegetable milks described in the recipe section (pp. 37-41). Use carob flour (sweet) to mask the bean flavor of commercial milk substitutes.

Teas China, India tea, or any variety of herb teas with lemon or Magic milk. These are best made in one pot, left to infuse for two minutes, then strained into a second heated pot. This method prevents stewing of the tea with release of tannin and caffeine, both of which are undesirable. Do not use instant tea.

YOU MAY EAT

Mid-day meal at home

Eggs As at breakfast. Do not eat often if using much Magic milk or Magic cream, which contain egg.

Fats Magic cream (recipe 83), vegetable oils (olive, peanut if grain- or gluten-free, safflower, soya, sunflower, but no corn), peanut butter (provided guaranteed grain- or gluten-free).

Fish Any variety—baked, boiled, fried, broiled, sautéed or steamed, with potato flour, paprika or soy flour for browning or under potato pastry (recipe 208).

Appetizers Anchovies, bacon, chicken livers, crab, mushrooms, roe on potato toast, salmon, sardines, shrimps (or other fish or shellfish) in brine or oil only. Oysters in bacon (nitrite-free and *not* sugar-cured), prunes in bacon. Any raw or cooked vegetables (except sweet corn) with oil or lemon or home-made mayonnaise (see recipes 223, 224, 225).

Meats Any cut of beef, chicken, duck guinea fowl, game hare, kid, lamb, mutton, pigeon, pork (cut off fat), rabbit, turkey, veal, venison. The meat may be baked, boiled, broiled, roasted or sautéed (without any flour except lentil, pea, potato or soya flour), in gravy, sauce or stuffing.

Soups Any home-made soup with no flour (except potato or soya flour) or forbidden fats. (See chapter 15.)

Sweet course Any fresh, dried or unsweetened canned fruit. Any puddings based on coconut, Magic cream, Magic milk, potato or soya flour (see chapter 7).

Vegetables Any raw vegetables served as a salad with homemade mayonnaise (recipes 223, 224, 225), or oil, lemon or pure apple cider vinegar. They may be eaten with any hot or cold dish. Any cooked vegetables (except sweet corn) baked, boiled, fried, broiled, roasted, sautéed or steamed without any butter, cheese or flour (except potato or soya flour) or milk. Eat plenty of cooked potatoes, unpeeled as far as possible.

Beverages As at breakfast.

Snacks at home

Foods Any dried fruits except those that are glazed with corn syrup (apple rings, apricots, bananas, cherries, dates, figs, pears, prunes, raisins), raw pumpkin, sesame or sunflower seeds. Any fresh fruits available. Any raw vegetables such as sticks of carrot, celery, beet, parsnip, radishes and so on. Any nuts, raw or roasted but without oil or salt. Any biscuits, cakes or confectionery listed in the recipe section (chapters 3-5). Any sandwiches made from potato flour loaf (recipe 28).

Drinks Anything from the list of drinks permitted at breakfast.

WHAT TO CHOOSE WHEN EATING OUT

Breakfast

Foods Poached (discard toast) or soft-boiled eggs left in the shell.

Drinks See chapter 2 on homemade beverages. Avoid restaurant teas and coffees. Use herb tea bags, available at health food stores.

Mid-day or evening meal

Foods	It is so difficult to know exactly what has been done to food, and what it contains, that it is simpler, always, to carry as many food items as possible, using thermos, picnic hamper (which is insulated) and ice packs or ice cubes. Ingredients in restaurants are becoming more and more processed, and therefore more hazardous to people on limited diets.
Appetizers	Any of those suggested for eating at home but avoid mayonnaise.
Soups	Consommé only.
Meats	Any of those listed for meals at home, sautéed, broiled or roasted.
Eggs	Boiled or poached. (Discard toast.)
Fish	Baked, steamed or broiled. Do not eat fish cooked in batter.
Vegetables	Any available plainly-cooked vegetables without sauce or butter, such as beans or brussels sprouts. Baked or boiled potatoes (but avoid mashed dried potatoes, which often contain powdered milk).
Salads	These must be dressed with oil and lemon juice only. Avoid sauces.
Sweet Course	Fruit, fresh or unsweetened canned, without cream.
Drinks	Any of those permitted at home that are available.

Snacks

Foods	Dried fruits, unroasted nuts, raw vegetables.

It is easy to carry any of those suggested for snacks at home in small packages.

Drinks If available, choose from those suggested for snacks at home, or bring your own herb tea bags and order hot water.

MEALS WHEN TRAVELING BY PUBLIC TRANSPORT

Boat, plane or train breakfast

Foods The choice is usually limited to bacon and eggs. It is possible to carry a wide-necked vacuum flask to keep your own supply of food hot.

Drinks Order hot water to use with your own herb tea bag, or carry an ordinary vacuum flask with your own choice of a permitted drink.

Boat, plane or train mid-day and evening meal
(Choose as for eating out.)

Snacks

Foods Carry snacks well-wrapped; potato flour loaf sandwiches or any home-made items from the recipes or dried fruits and shelled nuts.

Drinks Your own herb tea with hot water.

TRAVELING BY CAR

Wherever possible, carry a picnic basket stocked with items from the foods you *may* eat.

FOODS PERMITTED BUT NOT RECOMMENDED

The following foods, not being based on grain or milk, are allowable in a diet for mental patients but are undesirable from other points of view. You are therefore advised to reduce their use to a minimum.

Fats Drippings, "cooking" fats, lard, and suet have a high content of saturated fats.

Sweeteners White sugar, which is present in nearly all bottled drinks, including sweetened "health" drinks, and in the permitted confectionery, may be corn-based. Choose honey, blackstrap molasses or raw sugar, which supply minerals and vitamins. Use them very sparingly.

Thickeners Arrowroot and tapioca may be used but they supply only "empty" calories. Choose potato or soya flour in salty foods and agar-agar, a seaweed product high in minerals, in sweet foods.

SUPPLIES TO BE FOUND IN HEALTH FOOD STORES

Agar-agar; carob flour; chicory and dandelion coffee; herb teas; honey; nuts (fresh, unshelled); pure peanut butter; potato flour (free of powdered milk); split pea flour; sea salt; soya flour; vegetable oils (peanut, olive, safflower, sesame, or sunflower). Keep oils refrigerated after opening.

FORBIDDEN FOODS

Because the following foods contain some grain or grain constituent—wheat, oats, barley, rye, corn, millet, rice and/or some milk, milk constituent, or other dairy product, they should not be used.

All dairy- and grain-containing products, including: bagels, barley, biscuits, blancmange, bread, bread puddings, breadcrumbs, breading on fowl and seafood, breakfast cereals, bulghur, cake mixes, cakes, cheeses, cheese products, cheese-containing products, cookies, corn, corn flakes, corn grits, corn meal, corn syrup, cracker crumbs, crackers, cream desserts, crispbreads, crispies, croquettes, croutons, crumpets, custards (boiled, frozen, steamed), dextrose, doughnuts, dumplings, egg whites (dried), eggnog (commercial), flans, frozen desserts, fructose, fruitcakes, gelatin dessert mixes, gluten, gravies, gruenkern, griddlecakes, high fructose corn syrup, hot cakes, ice cream cones, ice cream (commercial, including so-called "health" ice creams and frozen flavored yogurt), ice milk, icings (commercial), infant feeding formulas, johnnycakes, junket, lemon curd, macaroni, malt, meatloaves, meat patties, meringues, millet, modified food starch, muesli, muffins, non-dairy creamers, noodles, pancakes, omelets (in restaurants they may contain milk or flour), pancake mixes, pasta, pastries, pie fillings, pies, pizzas, polenta, popovers, popcorn, porridge, pretzels, pumpernickel, puddings (boiled, milk, steamed), rolls, rusks, rye, spaghetti, scones, semolina, sherbets, sour dressing (served in restaurants over baked potatoes), shortbreads, soufflés, starch, starch-reduced rolls and cereals, tacos, tarts, timbales, toasts, toppings (commercial), trifles, turnovers, vermicelli, waffles, wheat cakes, wheat germ, wheat germ oil, yeast, zweiback

Soups creamed, packaged, dehydrated, pouched soups, now served in the majority of restaurants and other mass-feeding places, as well as commercially-available products at the retail level

Entrees fresh, frozen, canned or pouched meat products (including bacon, poultry, and seafood) with any grain flour as coating, filler, binder, pastry, stuffing, or thickener; meat in commercial gravies, soups or stews which may have been thickened with grain flour; commercial black pudding, cervelat, chop suey, chow mein, cold cuts, croquettes, forcemeats, frankfurters, galantines, haggis, hamburger extenders, hamburgers, head cheese, hot dogs, Lebanon bologna, liverwurst, luncheon meats, meat loaves, minces, pasties, pastries (meat), pork and beans, pork roll, ravioli, salami, scrapple, sausages, weiners

Vegetables vegetable mixes, sweet corn, vegetarian canned or boxed foods containing gluten or caseinate (check labels carefully)

Sauces	commercial sauces of many varieties (soy sauce, for example, may consist of 50 percent wheat)
Condiments	bouillon cubes; celery salt; curry powder; fruit: conserves, jellies, butters, preserves, jams; curry powder; garlic salt; mayonnaise; mustard (prepared); monosodium glutamate (MSG); olives; pepper (synthetic); pickles (commercial); seasoned salt; vinegar (except pure apple cider vinegar)
Fats & Oils	butter, cheeses, corn oil, cream, margarines (some contain milk fractions), oleomargarines, "vegetable oils" or "blended oils" without specification about their derivations; flavoring extracts
Sweets & Confections	butterscotch, candies, caramels, carob-containing candies, chewing gums, chocolate-containing candies, chocolates, creams, fondants, fudge, Lifesavers, lollipops, licorice, marzipan, sourballs, toffees
Beverages (Alcoholic)	ale, beer, brandy, gin (grain and cane spirits), malt liquor, liqueur, rum, stout, tequila, whiskey (Bourbon, Canadian, Irish, Scotch, and blends of all aforementioned), wine (grape, sherry, vermouth)
Beverages (Non-alcoholic)	chocolate drink, chocolate mix, cocoa, cocoa mix, cocomalt, coffee (concentrate, instant, substitute), cola drinks, cream soda, lemonade mix, malted milk, milk (fluid, non-fat dried, evaporated, condensed), Ovaltine, root beer, soft drinks, tomato juice (commercial), bottled cloudy beverages

Non-food Items That May Contain Corn Fractions

Consumer goods	adhesives (envelopes, stamps, stickers, tapes); starched garments (skin contacts); fumes inhaled while cooking corn or corn products, or while ironing starch-treated garments, may induce adverse reactions in corn-sensitive persons.
Medications	aspirins; breath sprays and drops; birth control

pills; cough syrups; diluents and excipients (used in lozenges, ointments, supplements, suppositories, tablets)

Toiletries dentifrices, hair sprays, powders (body and face), toothpaste and toothpowders

*****

Testing for possible food or drink allergies

You may be one of those people who are sensitive to some food or drink not listed among the Forbidden Foods. Here is a simple method of finding out what this substance or substances may be.

1. Take none of the suspected food or drink for 5 days.

2. Then take *nothing but* this substance at one meal, preferably your last one in the evening, and wait to see if you have an unpleasant reaction to it.

3. If you do have one, put it on your "To be avoided list" or use another recipe which does not contain it.

4. If you don't have one carry on including it in your diet and test some other food or drink in the same way.

Warning It has been stated by Dr. Theron Randolph, the well known allergist, that allergic type responses to foods develop to those dietary items which are used most frequently and consistently, which is the reason why cereal grains and milk products head the lot. Substitutions for eggs, potato, soya and other foods encourage the spread of intolerances to such substitutes, unless a warning is given that *no dietary item should be used more frequently than once in four or more days*.

Importance of diversity in foods To ensure the largest choice within the necessary limitations imposed by the exclusion of all grains and milk products, a very wide range of permissible ingredients has been used, and many differing recipes are given.

Substitutes for certain foods which may be allergens

1. Fats. Use any vegetable oil (except corn), ringing changes on peanuts, olive, safflower, sesame, soy and sunflower.

2. Eggs. Eat chestnuts (198) in place of boiled eggs and toasted nuts (pages 41-43) to replace other sorts of cooked eggs. As binding agent replace each egg by 1 tsp. pectin, ½ tsp. baking powder-grain free (197) mixed with 1 tbs. water. Use ½ tbs. soya flour to replace 1 egg yolk used alone.

3. Potato, sweet potato, soya, split pea, lentil and carob flour are interchangeable.

4. All ground or chopped meat recipes can be varied, i.e. lamb, beef, pork, poultry, rabbit, etc.

Dried fruits

If not sun-dried, rinse well in colander under cold water tap to remove sulphur dioxide or mineral oil.

Medications and supplements

Although sticking to a milk-free grain-free diet is basic, this alone is not enough. Your family doctor will prescribe medication. Ask him also to approve of the following supplements:

Nicotinamide (vitamin B-3), 1 gram three times daily
Ascorbic acid (vitamin C), 1 gram three times daily

One *mixed vitamin and mineral* tablet daily
These can be obtained at your health store. Be absolutely certain that the supplements are free of grain, additives or coloring.

Chapter 2

BEVERAGES

COLD DRINKS

People who own a blender will find the following cold drinks made from fruits both health-giving and delicious. After liquidizing the fruit the pulp may be strained off but since all fruit pulp is valuable nutritionally, greater benefit will be gained by continuing to liquidize until the pulp is as finely divided as possible so that it may remain in the drink which will, of course, then be slightly "thicker."

Cold drinks should be chilled but not served ice cold or digestion will be delayed until the stomach contents warm up again.

(1) **Apple Ambrosia**

2 cups unsweetened pineapple juice
2 cored and chopped tart apples
honey to taste

Put the juice in the blender and turn on. Add the apple gradually and blend until smooth. Taste, add honey if desired, and turn on again to blend thoroughly. Serve chilled in tall glasses.

(2) **Apple and Cucumber Shake**

2 cups cold water
1 cup sweet apples, cored and quartered
½ cup diced cucumber
2 tbs. lemon juice

Put the water into the blender and gradually add the other

ingredients, blending until smooth. Chill and serve in tall glasses.

(3) Apple and Banana Shake (serves one)

1 cup water
1 banana (really ripe) chopped
1 apple, washed, cored and quartered

Liquidize all ingredients in blender until smooth. Strain, chill and serve in a tall glass.

(4) Apple and Mint Shake (serves one)

1 cup cold water
1 tbs. honey
1 sweet apple, cored and quartered
1 small handful fresh mint leaves (washed)
squeeze of lemon juice

Put the water and honey into the blender. Start it running. Gradually add the apple, mint, and lemon juice, run for about twenty seconds. Stop and inspect the contents. If they are not well blended repeat the blending. Pour through a hair sieve, pressing out any pulp with a wooden spoon. Chill and serve in a tall glass.

(5) Apricot Delight

½ cup dried apricots
boiling water to cover
1 tbs. honey
2 cups water
a little lemon juice (optional)

Pour enough boiling water over the apricots to cover them well and leave them to soak overnight. Cook them gently in the same water with the honey until quite soft. Add two cups of water with a squeeze of lemon juice and liquidize in blender until smooth. Chill and serve in tall glasses.

(6) Banana Shake

1 banana
1 tsp. clear honey
1 cup soya milk (73)
1 cup cold water

Cut the banana into several pieces and put them in the blender, add the honey and soya milk and mix well in blender. Chill and serve in a tall glass with a straw.

(Scraped vanilla bean or almond butter (see pp. 41-42) or cinnamon may be substituted for banana or a few dried apricots soaked overnight in sufficient water to cover).

(7) **Berry Milk Shake**

1 cup strawberries, raspberries blackberries, etc.
1 tsp. honey
1 tbs. lemon juice
pinch of salt
3 to 4 cups soya milk (73)

Liquidize, chill and serve in tall glasses.

(8) **Carob Shake** (serves one)

1 to 2 tsp. carob flour
1 tbs. cold water
scant cup soya milk (73)
pinch of scraped vanilla bean (if desired)

Make a smooth paste with the water and carob flour. Add it to the soya milk and pour the mixture into a blender with the vanilla. Blend well until frothy and serve in a tall glass.

(9) **Coconut Milk Shake** (serves one)

½ cup coconut milk
1 small apple, cored and quartered
1 slice peeled raw young beet (diced)

Pour the coconut milk into a blender and turn on. Gradually add the apple quarters and raw beet and blend until quite smooth. It should not need further sweetening. Serve chilled in a tall glass.

(11) **Elderberry Shake**

1 cup elderberries (fresh or bottled)
2 cups water
squeeze of lemon juice to taste

Liquidize in blender, strain, chill and serve in tall glasses.

(12) **Golden Shake** (serves one)

1 cup water
½ cup shredded celery
½ cup grated carrot
2 to 3 tbs. orange juice

Put the water in the blender. Turn on, gradually add the other ingredients and blend until smooth. Strain through a hair sieve (reserving the pulp for a soup or stew), chill and serve in a tall glass.

(13) **Lemonade** (sweet, without sugar)

½ lb. seedless raisins
2 pints cold water
juice of 2 lemons, unstrained
1 tbs. honey

Blend the raisins in a blender with half a pint of the water or mince very finely. Add the rest of the water and bring to the boil. Leave overnight. Next day, press through a fine sieve. Add the lemon juice and honey and mix well. Chill.

(14) **Lemon Delight**

2 small lemons
1 cup chopped celery heart
2 cups cold water
honey to taste

Squeeze all the juice from the lemons. Put the water in the blender and turn on. Add the other ingredients gradually and blend until fine and smooth. Chill and serve in tall glasses.

(15) **Lemon Tea** (serves one)

½ pint boiling water
½ tsp. tea leaves (24)
2 tbs. lemon juice
honey to taste

Pour the boiling water on to the tea. Let it stand for two minutes then strain and add the lemon juice and honey. Chill and serve in a glass.

N.B. With this method there is no bitterness as there is when lemon slices are used with the pith on.

(16) **Orange Shake (plain)**

2 oranges, peeled, seeded and quartered
2 cups water
1 tsp. honey

Liquidize the ingredients until smooth or whisk thoroughly. Chill and serve in tall glasses. (Strain or sieve if desired but the pulp is pleasant and nutritious).

(The same recipe may be used for lemon shake, adding more honey).

(17) **Orange and Ginger Shake**

2 oranges peeled, seeded and quartered
2 cups cold water
squeeze of lemon juice
½ tsp. ground ginger

Blend until smooth, chill and serve in tall glasses.

(18) **Orange and Mint Shake** (serves one)

½ orange
½ cup cold water
a few leaves of fresh mint

Peel the orange, quarter it and remove the seeds. Add the flesh to the water with the mint leaves. Blend till very fine, stopping and starting as required. Chill and serve in a tall glass.

(19) **Spicy Soya Milk Shake**

4 cups soya milk (73)
½ tsp. grated or ground nutmeg
good pinch of sea salt
½ tsp. ground ginger
sprinkle of cinnamon

Blend well and serve chilled in tall glasses, sprinkled with cinnamon if desired.

(20) **"Strawberry" Shake**

1 small young raw beet
1 small sweet apple
1 can unsweetened pineapple juice
1 ripe banana (optional)

Wash, peel and dice the beet and core the apple. Pour half the juice into the blender and run for a couple of seconds with the cover on. Remove the lid and gradually add the apple and beet pieces. When smooth add the rest of the juice. For extra smoothness include one chopped ripe banana and liquidize all together. To sweeten further a dash of clear honey may be added.

(21) **Tomato Juice**

2 cups water
2 cups chopped tomatoes, fresh or canned
1 shallot or very small onion
pinch of basil or marjoram
dash of honey

Blend all ingredients in blender until smooth. Strain, reserving the pulp for gravy etc., and serve.

(22) **Very Special Soya Milk Shake**

4 cups soya milk (73)
3 to 4 tbs. molasses
1 tbs. roasted ground almonds (see p. 41-42)

Blend all ingredients and serve in tall glasses, chilled.

HOT DRINKS

Here are some alternative hot beverages to coffee. Beware of all coffee substitutes. Except for dandelion coffee (which is recommended) they are made of grains either alone or mixed with roasted vegetable beans.

Herbal Teas

Health food stores keep a range of herb teas. If you are not already accustomed to drinking them, it is a good idea to buy a sample of each in turn to find which suit your fancy. Most herbs can be grown easily in the garden or in a pot on the kitchen window sill to give a supply of fresh leaves. They should be picked with discretion so that no plant is picked bare, which would destroy it. The basic recipe for all herbal teas is as follows:

(24) **Herb Tea** (serves one)

1 tsp. or more to taste of leaves or flowers
1 cup boiling water

Put the leaves in a clean, wide-mouthed jug. Pour on boiling water, turn into a pan and simmer for one minute. Take off the heat and let the leaves steep for a few minutes. Pour through a strainer into a heated teacup and drink plain or with lemon juice. (Steeping for too long makes the brew bitter.) Herb teas make ideal drinks for a milk-free diet since they are always drunk without milk. If sweetening is desired use a little honey to taste.

Carob—The Cocoa Substitute

Cocoa powder, since it has white flour added to it, is forbidden but carob flour is permitted. This is the ground-up pod of the algarroba bean of Spain and Spanish America where it is fed to donkeys and horses and is also much appreciated by chewing children who know it as "donkey's chocolate." Use it as follows to take the place of chocolate drinks.

(25) **Donkey's Chocolate** (serves one)

1 to 2 tsp. carob flour
2 tbs. cold water
scant cup soya milk (73) or Magic milk (77)
pinch of scraped vanilla bean (optional)

Put the carob flour into a cup. Add the water and mix to a smooth paste. Put the soya milk in a wetted pan and bring it to a boil. Pour it over the paste and stir well. Return the liquid to the pan, add vanilla and re-heat, stirring well.

(26) **Egg Flip** (serves one)

1 egg yolk
¾ cup soya milk (73)
vanilla bean or almond butter (see pp. 41-42) to taste
1 tbs. honey

Beat the yolk in a bowl, adding the desired flavoring. Heat the milk, keeping it below boiling point, and stir in the honey. Pour the mixture over the yolk, stirring well. Drink at once.

(27) **Savory Milk Shake** (serves one)

½ cup soya milk (73)
½ cup warm water
½ to 1 tsp. yeast extract

Whisk or blend together. Heat up and drink hot.

Chapter 3

BISCUITS, BREAD, SCONES

(28) **Potato Bread**

1 tsp. dry yeast granules
1 tsp. raw sugar
4 oz. lukewarm water
4 oz. potato flour
2 heaped tsp. soya flour
¼ tsp. sea salt
1 tbs. oil
1 egg, lightly whisked

Preheat oven to 400°F.
Cream the yeast with the raw sugar, add one ounce of the water and leave to froth. Mix and sieve the potato flour, soya flour and salt. Roughly add the oil—not corn! (If it is too carefully rubbed there is less flour available to be used by the yeast.) Add the egg and mix to a thick batter (like a sponge mixture). Place in an oiled and "floured" tin (use potato flour). Allow to rise to double the size (this will take about fifteen minutes if the tin is placed in a plastic bag). Cook at 400°F. for fifteen minutes then turn down the heat to 350° for fifteen to twenty minutes more. When the loaf is brown and firm turn it out onto a cooling rack.

(29) **Potato Drop Scones (English)**

2 cups potato flour
pinch of sea salt
½ tsp. bicarbonate of soda
1 tsp. cream of tartar
1 egg
½ tsp. honey
water

Sieve the dry ingredients. Drop in the egg and honey and mix rapidly to a smooth paste, adding enough water to make a very thick batter. Oil a griddle and heat it. Drop small rounds of batter onto it from a tablespoon. When bubbles rise from the surface of the scones turn with a spatula and cook the other side until brown and sides look dry.

(30) **Potato Flatties**

3 cups leftover mashed potato	1 beaten egg
pinch of sea salt	pinch of mixed herbs (optional)

Mix all ingredients well together. Shape into flat cakes about half an inch thick and place them on a hot griddle brushed with oil. When the bottoms are brown turn the cakes with a spatula to brown the other side. Eat hot with chopped chives.

(31) **Potato Flour Biscuits**

⅓ cup oil (*never* corn)	½ tsp. sea salt
1½ cups potato flour	1 egg

Preheat oven to 225-250°F.
Blend oil and the potato flour, add the salt and well beaten egg. Roll the mixture out thinly, cut it into small biscuits and bake them for about twelve to eighteen minutes in a very slow oven at 225-250°F. Turn the biscuits onto a wire tray to cool and store them in an airtight container when cold.

(32) **Potato Savory Droppies**

4 tbs. raw old potatoes, coarsely grated	1 heaped tbs. grated raw onion
juice of 1 lemon	1 egg

After grating the potatoes, squeeze out the moisture between towelling, transfer the pulp to a dish and cover it with the strained lemon juice. Wring out the grated onion in towelling and put it into a small bowl. Break the egg into this and beat together. Heat a griddle or heavy frying pan over a low heat until it sizzles when brushed with oil. Squeeze the potatoes dry again and beat into the contents of the bowl. Drop tablespoonfuls of the mixture wide apart on to the hot griddle (or frying pan) and spread out into thin neat rounds. When the surfaces bubble turn the droppies with a spatula and cook to the same rich brown on the other side. Serve hot with any savory spread (see chapter 16).

(33) **Potato Scones (British)**

1 lb. hot cooked potatoes (3 medium)
sea salt to taste
1 tbs. oil
4 tbs. lentil or soya flour

Mash the potatoes in a mixing bowl and add the sea salt, oil and the flour. Beat to a dough. Roll out on a lentil-floured board to one-quarter-inch thickness. Cut into small rounds and bake on a hot oiled griddle or frying pan. Turn the scones when brown and brown the other side. Serve hot.

(34) **Potato Scones (Irish)**

2 cups mashed potato
a little oil
1 egg
potato flour as required

Steam the potatoes in their jackets. Peel and mash them and measure two cupfuls. Mix in the oil and beaten egg and add enough potato flour to stiffen the dough. Roll out and cut into rounds. Bake on a hot griddle or in the oven until golden brown. Serve hot with a savory spread or meat or vegetable extract.

(35) **Potato Scones (Scottish)**

1 cup cooked potato
1 tbs. oil
sea salt
about 3 tbs. potato flour

Mash the potatoes with the oil in a bowl, adding salt to taste. Turn onto a board spread with potato flour. Rub in as much potato flour as the potato will absorb and work the mixture into a pliable dough. Roll out as thin as possible, bake on a hot griddle (or heavy frying pan) and prick all over with a fork. Cook for three minutes on each side. Wrap in a clean cloth to cool.

(36) Spice Biscuits

4 tbs. oil
4 tbs. honey
½ tsp. cinnamon
¼ tsp. ground ginger
¼ tsp. grated nutmeg
1 cup split pea flour
lemon juice

Preheat oven to 350°F.

Beat together the oil and honey, then heat slightly. Cool. Sift the spices with the split pea flour then add to the oil mixture to make a stiff dough. Add lemon juice if too stiff or more split pea flour if not stiff enough. Chill, roll out very thin. Preheat oven to 350°F. Cut into rounds with a wine glass or biscuit cutter and bake on an oiled pan for about fifteen minutes.

Breadless Open and Closed Sandwiches

Bread is forbidden to people on a grain-free diet so that they are unable to eat traditional sandwiches. But why do sandwiches have to be made using bread? Discard your prejudices and adopt some of the following ideas for sandwiches using other materials.

1. Meat Eaters

Thin slices of any cold meat, meat or liver loaf or head cheese, or cold chicken, spread with chopped cucumber, etc., bound with home-made mayonnaise or spread with peanut butter and slices of cucumber or finely chopped celery, parsley, etc.

2. Vegetarians

Use thin slices of peanut and potato loaf (314) or potato loaf (28) as above.

3. Anyone

(a) Use lettuce leaves or celery stalks in place of bread.
(b) Use thin slices of large hard apples in place of bread.
(c) Thin slivers of peanut or potato loaf spread with finely chopped parsley, or chopped chives or parsley with homemade mayonnaise or any desired mixture, or savory spread.

(37) **Uncooked Nut Fingers**

½ cup dried coconut
¼ cup (scant) oil
½ cup lightly roasted minced hazel nuts
½ cup crystalized honey
½ cup raisins
2 to 4 tbs. soya flour

Blend all ingredients in a bowl to the consistency of pastry dough, adding more soya flour if too moist. Pat into strips about one-and-a-half inches wide and half an inch deep on waxed paper. Cover with more waxed paper, then press down hard. Chill. Remove the paper carefully and leave the fingers in air to dry fully before using. (Any other nuts may be substituted.)

Chapter 4

CAKES

(38) **Almond Mounds**

½ cup ground almonds
1½ tbs. oil
2 tbs. honey
½ cup potato flour
1 egg
pinch of sea salt

Preheat oven to 350°F.
Blend the oil with the honey, almonds, potato flour and salt. Mix well with the beaten egg to form a stiff paste. Place in small cones on an oiled pan and bake in a moderate oven (350°F.) for about twenty minutes.

(39) **Carob Cake**

3 eggs
½ cup honey
½ cup oil
½ cup soya flour
½ cup carob flour

Preheat oven to 325°F.
Place the first three ingredients in the blender, liquidize and pour over the flours in a bowl. Mix well and bake on an oiled pan at 325°F. until done. (Soya, carob and honey burn easily.) Turn out onto a wire rack.

(40) **Cinnamon Drop Cakes**

⅓ cup oil
1 cup honey
2 eggs
2 cups potato flour
sprinkle of cinnamon

Preheat oven to 350°F.
Blend the oil and honey. Add the eggs one at a time beating well after each. When all is well beaten add the

flour to make a batter consistency. Line baking pans with paper and onto them drop spoonfuls of the mixture about the size of half walnuts about one-and-a-half inches apart. Dust with cinnamon and bake in a moderate oven (350°F.) until done.

(41) Coconut Brownies

8 tbs. dried coconut
6 tbs. honey
1 egg
potato flour as required

Preheat oven to 350°F.
Mix the coconut and honey thoroughly and add the well-beaten egg. Beat with a fork until the mixture sticks well together, adding potato flour as required to thicken. Drop from a tablespoon onto an oiled tin and bake in a moderate oven (350°F.) until golden brown and firm.

(42) Coconut Pyramids

1 lb. dried coconut
pinch of sea salt
2 tbs. potato flour (or more if required)
½ cup honey
1 white of egg
½ tsp. oil to brush baking tin

Preheat oven to 350°F.
Mix the coconut, salt, potato flour and honey and stir in the beaten egg white. Add enough potato flour to make a very stiff paste. Drop in spoonfuls onto an oiled baking tin and bake for fifteen minutes in a moderate oven (350°F.) or until the surface is golden brown.

(43) Coconut Rocks

1½ tbs. oil
3 tbs. honey
5 tbs. potato flour
3 tbs. dried coconut
1 egg
almond butter to taste (see pp. 41-42)

Preheat oven to 425°F.
Blend the oil and honey. Add the potato flour and coconut by degrees, then the egg and almond butter, still beating the mixture. Drop from a teaspoon onto an oiled baking pan and bake in a quick oven (425°F.) for about eight minutes.

(44) **Fig Toughies**

1 cup soya milk (73)
pinch of scraped vanilla bean
4 tbs. potato flour (or more if required)
1 cup chopped figs

Preheat oven to 325°F.

Mix well the first three ingredients then add the figs and mix thoroughly. Line a baking pan with paper and drop the mixture from a teaspoon onto this, spacing the droppings well apart. Bake at 325°F. for twelve to fifteen minutes. Remove from the paper while still hot. Minced raisins, apple rings or apricots may be used instead of figs.

(45) **Fruit Fingers** (uncooked)

½ cup raisins
½ cup shredded fresh coconut
½ cup shelled peanuts
½ cup pitted dates
½ cup chopped raw apple
1 banana
lemon juice if required
soya flour as required

Put all the ingredients except the soya flour through a mincer or blender and turn into a bowl. Stir in enough soya flour to make a dryish mixture and mix thoroughly. Taste and add a few drops of lemon juice if too sweet. Lay a piece of waxed paper on a flat dish and spread the mixture smoothly over it with a spatula. Cover with a piece of waxed paper and press well down. Chill. Strip off the paper and cut the mixture into fingers with a sharp knife, or roll it into walnut-sized balls.

(46) **Honey Fruit Cake**

⅞ cup oil
2 eggs
2 cups potato flour
1 cup raisins
1 cup honey
juice and rind of 1 lemon
a few chopped almonds
a grating of nutmeg

Preheat oven to 350°F.

Blend the oil and eggs, one by one, followed by the rest of the ingredients. Bake in an oiled pan, lined with parchment paper, in a moderate oven (350°F.) until done.

(47) Large Lemon Potato Cake

4 cups (1 lb.) potato flour
⅞ cup oil
1 egg (or 2 whites)
½ tsp. lemon juice
1 cup honey

Preheat oven to 400°F.
Mix all the ingredients and beat well for ten minutes. Pour into an oiled cake pan and bake in a rather quick oven (400°F.) for about fifteen minutes.

(48) Lemon Kisses

1½ tbs. oil
4 tbs. raw sugar
3 eggs
few drops lemon juice
grated rind of ½ lemon
4 tbs. arrowroot

Preheat oven to 350°F.
Blend the oil and raw sugar to a soft cream. Whisk the eggs for five minutes, add to the mixture and beat until smooth. Add the lemon juice and rind and stir in the arrowroot. Put spoonfuls of the mixture into oiled shallow patty pans and bake in a moderate oven (350°F.) for ten minutes.

(49) Lunch Cake

pinch sea salt
2 cups potato flour
⅓ cup oil
½ cup honey
1 cup molasses
1 cup dried fruit (raisins, dates, peel, etc.)
½ tsp. mixed spices
1 tsp. bicarbonate of soda
½ to ¾ cup soya milk
1 tbs. cider vinegar
1 tbs. raw sugar

Preheat oven to 300°F.
Crush the sea salt and sift with potato flour. Add the oil and honey, molasses, fruit and spice. Dissolve the bicarbonate of soda in a little of the soya milk and add the rest of the milk to the mixture to make a stiff dough. Add the vinegar, raw sugar and bicarbonate in milk, beating in well. Put into a well-oiled pan lined with oiled brown paper and bake in a slow oven (300°F.) for one-and-a-half to two hours according to the depth of the cake.

(50) **Macaroons (plain)**

½ cup ground almonds
½ cup soya flour
½ cup (scant) honey
3 egg whites, lightly beaten

Preheat oven to 300°F.

Mix the almonds, soya flour and honey. Fold in the egg whites. Shape into balls about one-and-a-half inches across. Place onto parchment paper on a baking sheet and bake in a slow oven (300°F.) for ten to fifteen minutes.

(51) **Macaroons (special)**

½ cup honey
½ cup blanched and ground almonds
2 egg whites
1 tbs. lemon juice
a few whole almonds, blanched

Preheat oven to 300°F.

Mix the honey and the ground almonds. Beat the egg whites until they form stiff peaks, then stir them into the almond mixture. Add the lemon juice. Drop in small portions onto parchment paper on a baking pan and bake in a slow oven (300°F.) for about twenty minutes. When nearly done put half an almond on to the center of each macaroon.

(52) **Macaroons (on apple)**

2 egg whites
4 tbs. honey
4 tbs. ground almonds
1 tbs. soya flour
cooked apple flavored with grated lemon rind

Preheat oven to 425°F.

Beat the egg whites until quite stiff. Gently fold in the honey, ground almonds, and soya flour. Cut small rounds of greaseproof paper. Set a teaspoonful of cooked apple on each and cover with a tablespoonful of the almond mixture. Bake in a hot oven (425°F.) for about ten to fifteen minutes.

(53) **Merry Macaroons**

2 eggs
½ cup honey
1 cup potato flour
1 tsp.(scant) oil
pinch of sea salt
1 tsp. lemon juice
nearly 3 cups shredded coconut

Preheat oven to 325°F.

Beat the eggs until they foam. Add the honey slowly and beat for about five minutes until thickened. Add the potato flour slowly then beat in the margarine, flavoring and coconut. Drop teaspoonfuls of the mixture onto a baking pan and bake at 325°F. for about fifteen minutes or until brown around the edges. Cool slightly before removing. For special occasions garnish when cool with toasted shelled and skinned peanuts.

(54) **Soya Cake**

3 eggs
¾ cup honey
¾ cup oil
⅛ tsp. scraped vanilla bean
1 tbs. almond butter (see pp. 41-42)
1 cup soya flour
1 tbs. cream of tartar

Preheat oven to 325-350°F.
Blend the eggs, honey, oil and flavorings in the blender, add to the dry ingredients in a bowl and stir well. Pour the mixture into an oiled cake pan and bake at 325-350°F. until done. (Better slow and long than fast and short.)

(55) **Sponge Cake**

4 eggs, separated
1 cup honey
2 tbs. lemon juice
⅛ tsp. sea salt
1 scant cup potato flour

Preheat oven to 325°F.
Beat the egg yolks until thick. Blend in the honey, lemon juice and salt. Fold in portions of potato flour and stiffly beaten egg whites alternately. Turn the mixture into an oiled nine-inch pan and bake at 325°F. for about twenty minutes, then raise the heat to (350°F.) and continue baking for fifteen to twenty minutes longer or until done.

(56) **Unbaked Fruit Cake**

1 cup minced seedless raisins
1 cup shredded coconut
2 tbs. lemon juice
grated rind of ½ lemon
1 cup chopped nuts
1 cup chopped pitted dates
½ cup chopped or diced fresh or dried bananas
enough carob flour to absorb moisture

Mix thoroughly all ingredients except the carob flour. Add the carob flour as required. Press the mixture into a lightly oiled loaf pan and chill. Turn out onto a plate and slice thinly with a very sharp knife dipped in hot water.

(57) **Vanilla Cake**

3 eggs
4 tbs. honey
¼ inch scraped vanilla bean
½ cup oil
1 cup potato flour (unsifted)
1 tbs. home-made baking powder (197)

Preheat oven to 325°F.

Liquidize in a blender the first four ingredients and pour over the dry ingredients in a bowl, stirring well. Bake at 325°F. until done.

Chapter 5

CONFECTIONERY

(to be eaten in strict moderation)

(58) **Brown Nougat**

½ lb. sweet almonds
1 lb. raw sugar
1 lemon
a little oil

Blanch and shred the almonds finely. Toast in a moderate oven until hot but not brown. Put the sugar in a pan with two tablespoonfuls of lemon juice and stir with a wooden spoon over quite a gentle heat until the sugar is dissolved. Stir briskly and boil to 240°F. using a sugar thermometer to check the temperature. Add the almonds and mix well. Pour onto an oiled dish, press out with a spatula and cut into bars. If liked, parchment paper may be used round the bars.

(59) **Carob Fudge**

2 tbs. honey
1 to 2 tbs. oil
2 tbs. or more carob flour

Mix all ingredients well together and then beat well. Press the mixture into an oiled rectangular pan and cut into squares. Chill.

(60) **Coconut Balls**

1 cup coconut meal (unsweetened)
½ cup pitted dates, figs or raisins
carob flour as required

Grind the coconut very fine. Mince the dried fruit. Put

both in a bowl and knead into a dough. If too moist thicken with carob flour. Shape into small balls. If liked, coat by rolling in some of the coconut reserved for the purpose. Chill.

(61) **Fruities**

½ cup pitted dates, raisins or dried figs
½ cup fresh broken nuts
1 grated apple
1 tbs. lemon or orange juice
¼ to ½ cup soya flour

Put all ingredients in a bowl and mix thoroughly to a firm dry paste. Add a little more soya flour if too moist or a little less if too dry. Press down firmly on a small sheet of waxed paper to half-an-inch thickness. Chill thoroughly. Cut into small fingers about two inches by half an inch. Keep in a closed container.

(62) **Honey Squares**

½ cup honey
½ cup molasses
½ cup 100 percent peanut butter
1 cup soya flour
½ cup seedless raisins
scraped vanilla bean to taste

Put all the ingredients in a bowl and mix thoroughly. Knead on a board until the mixture is very stiff, adding soya flour if required. Cut into small squares after pressing out thinly. The squares may be rolled in a little raw sugar or dried coconut to coat.

(63) **Honey Toffee**

1 tbs. oil
1 cup honey
a little lemon juice

Pour the oil into a pan and shake to coat the surface. Put in the honey and lemon juice and cook, stirring constantly, until a soft ball forms when half a teaspoonful of the mixture is dropped into a cup of cold water. Pour into a well oiled pan and leave to set hard, then break in pieces using a light hammer over a clean dish towel.

(64) **Nut Crunch Fingers**

1 cup hazel nuts, peanuts, pecans or walnuts
1 tbs. lemon juice
2 tbs. crystalized honey
soya flour to thicken

Roast the nuts lightly then break them into pieces by covering with a clean cloth and tapping gently with a small hammer. Mix the broken nuts, lemon juice and honey well in a bowl and stir in enough soya flour to make a thick paste. Press into a flat dish brushed with oil and leave for a few days to harden. Chill, then cut into fingers.

(65) **Nut Toffee**

2 cups chopped nuts
1½ tbs. oil
2 cups honey
soya flour to thicken

Toast the nuts lightly then spread over an oiled pan. In a heavy pan heat the oil gently, then add the honey and stir until well blended. Add enough soya flour to thicken. Heat up again and pour hot over the nuts. Allow to cool and break up with a small hammer.

(66) **Peanut Butter Balls** (uncooked)

½ cup gluten-free peanut butter
½ cup honey
½ cup soya flour
1 tbs. lemon peel, chopped finely or pulverized

Mix all ingredients together and shape into small balls. Roll in shredded coconut, ground nuts or sesame seeds as desired.

(67) **Peanut Butter Fudge** (uncooked)

½ cup 100 percent peanut butter
½ cup honey
1 cup or so soya flour
cinnamon, lemon juice or vanilla bean flavoring

Combine the first two ingredients then stir in the soya flour and mix well to form a stiff paste. Add the flavoring, turn onto waxed paper and press down to half an inch thickness. Cut into cubes or roll into finger thickness. Chill and cut into chunks or stuff into pitted prunes or between halves of dried apricots, peaches or walnuts. Or roll into small balls and dust with coconut meal or milled nuts.

(68) **Peppermint Candy** (no milk)

12 tbs. honey
¾ glass water
1 tsp. peppermint extract

Put the honey and water in a pan and stir until the honey is dissolved, then bring to a boil. Raise to 240°F. (use a candy thermometer). Stir in the extract and turn the mixture into a bowl. Beat until thick, turn into an oiled dish or pan and cut into small squares when nearly cold.

(69) **Turkish Delight**

½ oz. agar-agar
¼ pint water
½ lb. clear honey
juice of 1 lemon, strained

Soak the agar-agar in half the water. Bring the rest of the water to a boil, add the honey and stir until it dissolves. Then add the agar-agar and continue stirring until it is quite dissolved. Simmer for twenty minutes and add the lemon juice. Rinse a flat dish with cold water and pour in the mixture to a depth of not more than one inch. Cut into cubes when cold.

(70) **Walnut Wonders**

½ cup raisins
½ cup pitted dates
½ cup pitted prunes
2 tbs. soya flour
6 walnuts

Mince the raisins, dates and prunes. Make into a stiff mixture by stirring in the soya flour, adding more if necessary. Roll into small balls and set on a plate to dry, or flatten down in an oiled pan and cut into squares. Press one piece of walnut on each.

Chapter 6

DAIRY PRODUCT SUBSTITUTES

It has been stated that "there is no evidence that milk, cheese or yogurt are necessary for adults." Indeed, man is the only adult animal of any species who consumes milk, a food designed for the very young.

Unfortunately westerners, accustomed to animal milk and its products from infancy, generally find plant substitutes (usually based on soya bean) unacceptable. This is on account of the unaccustomed "bean" flavor. However, a number of milk substitutes based on nuts have also been devised and these may be found more acceptable.

Another alternative is Magic milk which is based on egg and has a particularly delicate flavor. It can be used in tea and over fruit. Recipes for these are given below. Both Magic milk and soya milk are used as ingredients in the recipes in other sections. Manufacturers of certain commercial brands of soya milk have tried to make their products more palatable by adding malt to mask the "bean" flavor. Such milks must not be used by anyone on a grain-free diet since malt is made from barley.

However, a method of making soya milk at home has been worked out which eliminates the strong bean flavor. The following recipe for making it is used by kind permission of the publishers, Woodbridge Press Publishing Co., Santa Barbara, U.S.A.

Extract from "The Oats, Peas, Beans & Barley Cookbook" by Edyth Young Cottrell, Research Nutritionist, Loma Linda University, California. Published by Woodbridge

Press Publishing Co., Santa Barbara, California 93111, U.S.A. (Copyright © 1974 by Edyth Young Cottrell).

SOYA MILK (HOME MADE)

"Forget any old ideas you may have about 'bean taste' in the new soybean products. Cornell University has developed a method for eliminating the strong bean flavor in making soy milk directly from the soybeans—any variety may be used. Formerly only the mildest flavored beans were selected for making milk and even so there was a characteristic soybean flavor. Careful study disclosed that as soon as the bean was broken the enzyme action began to produce the strong flavor. By blending in very hot water the enzymes were inactivated as fast as the beans were broken and so no strong flavor developed. This method is well-adapted to home use.

One pound of beans may produce three and one-half to four quarts of soy milk with approximately the same amount of protein as dairy milk—at a cost only slightly higher than the price of the beans.

(71) **Soybean Concentrate**

"Equipment and procedure

Blender
Large kettles
Large double boiler
Shallow bowl
Colander
Measuring spoons
Rubber spatula
Large strainer
About 24" square of fine mesh nylon curtain material.

The following ingredients

1 lb. soybeans
7 cups water (for soaking)
2 kettles of boiling water for preheating
4½ to 5 quarts of boiling water for blending.

"Sort and measure two-and-one-quarter cups (one pound) unbroken soybeans. Wash and soak in seven cups water from four to sixteen hours. Have ready large kettles of boiling water. Drain beans. Sort out beans which have been broken while soaking. Fill top of blender with hottest water from tap and let stand. Measure one and one-half cups sorted, soaked beans into flat bowl or pan. Set bowl of beans in sink. Let hottest water from tap fill bowl and continue to run slowly over beans.

"Empty top of blender and fill with boiling water. Drain beans in colander or strainer. Pour water from blender over beans in strainer. Put hot beans into hot blender. Cover with two cups boiling water. Put lid on securely, place thick hot pads or folded towel on top. Cover with folded plastic. Press down firmly on cover while starting blender or steam may cause water to spurt out. Blend two to three minutes at high speed.

"Caution: Do not allow children around while working with boiling water.

"To this point the process for making Soy Milk, Concentrated Soy Milk and Soybean Concentrate is the same—only the proportions of water are different. For Soybean Concentrate, empty the slurry (blended soybeans) into a pan.

SOY MILK AND CONCENTRATED SOY MILK

(72) **Concentrated Soy Milk**

"Follow method for making Soy Milk except use one-half the amount of water or less.

(73) **Soy Milk**

"Use concentrate as prepared above.

Place large strainer over deep kettle or bowl. Put square of nylon curtain material over strainer. Pour slurry (blended soybean concentrate) into cloth-lined strainer. Gather up edges of strainer-cloth in fingers and twist. Press lightly with rubber spatula.

"Empty contents of strainer-cloth back into blender. Add two cups cold water. Blend briefly. Pour again into cloth-lined strainer. Twist strainer-cloth and squeeze with hands until most of liquid is extracted. (Some sediment will come through mesh. This will settle to bottom and milk can be drained off.)

"Pour into top of a large double boiler. (If a large double boiler is not available, improvise by setting a large pan in a large kettle.) Repeat process until all of the beans are used. Heat pan of soy milk over large kettle of boiling water, twenty to thirty minutes.

"Cool quickly by emptying boiling water and filling bottom of double boiler with cold water and setting container of soy milk over the cold water. Set in refrigerator to chill.

To flavor/fortify Soy Milk. This step is of extreme importance and may need to be worked out to suit individual or family tastes. Flavorings commonly used and amounts per quart are:

Oil	1 tablespoon
Salt	⅛ teaspoon
Pure honey	2 tablespoons
Vitamin B12	Dissolve one 50mg*/tablet of vitamin B12 in two tablespoons of hot water. Stir. Use one teaspoon of liquid per quart.

"Blend one quart of milk at a time, add oil gradually. Add flavorings. The milk is now ready to serve. It is essential that people on a total vegetarian diet have a dependable source of vitamin B12. *It should be used to fortify all soy milk products*."

The milk will keep for about four days in the refrigerator.

(74) **Coconut Milk (1)**

4 cups shredded coconut
4 cups warm water
honey to taste
dash of lemon juice
pinch of sea salt

Liquidize all ingredients in a blender and strain off the pulp, reserving it for fruit salads, curries, or puddings. Use the milk in cooking sweet dishes.

*This should read one 50 mcg tablet—H.C.H.

(75) **Coconut Milk (2)**

¼ lb. finely grated coconut
5 oz. boiling water

Pour the boiling water over the grated coconut. Leave to infuse for twenty minutes then strain and use. The "milk" produced by this method has a far better flavor than that found in the coconut but is rather sweet for pudding so add no sweetening agent. Use fresh coconut as the flavor of milk made with dried coconut is inferior.

(76) **Filbert (hazelnut) Milk** (serves one)

handful of filberts in shells
1 cup apple juice
1 tsp. honey (optional)

Shell the filberts and liquidize them in the blender with the apple juice. Chill and serve with a straw in a tall glass.

(77) **Magic Milk**

3 eggs lightly poached in 1 cup water (or 3 raw egg yolks)
½ cup oil
3 to 4 cups water

(N.B. The eggs are cooked because raw egg white steals the biotin part of the vitamin B complex).

Put the eggs into the blender with the oil and turn on. Add the water gradually. When full pour the mixture into a jug and add enough water to make two pints of milk. Label "Magic" (so as not to confuse it with cow's milk) and use wherever milk is used but whisk it up again first. It will keep in the refrigerator as long as cow's milk.

"BUTTERS" FROM ALMONDS, PEANUTS, PECANS, WALNUTS, ETC.

1. Toasting. (First step for almonds, pecans and walnuts.) Spread the shelled nuts out on a baking tin and roast at

350°F. for about fifteen minutes. Stir the nuts occasionally to ensure even roasting.
2. Grinding. (Second step.)
(a) With a hand mill. Adjust the mill to make the nuts come out as a firm paste but do not set it too tight. A hand mill may be used to grind a large quantity at a time.
(b) With an electric blender. Use the grinder or set at "grind." Only a few nuts should be ground at a time. Keep adding a little oil to make a paste.
At the end of the process mix in sea salt to taste and store the "butter" in clean airtight glass jars. The amount of salt required is generally about half a teaspoonful to one pound of butter. Keep any opened jar refrigerated.

(78) **Mixed Nut "Butter"**

½ cup filberts, shelled, skinned and chopped
½ cup peanuts, shelled, skinned and chopped
½ cup sesame seeds
½ cup almonds, blanched and slivered
oil as required
dribble of honey

Grind all ingredients to make a smooth paste. Scrape out and turn into a screw-topped jar. Keep refrigerated.

(79) **Mock "Butter" (savory)**

1 lb. mild white onions
1 tbs. oil
¼ tsp. sea salt
1 tbs. arrowroot
½ cup water

Peel and cut up the onions finely. Heat the oil in a pan and add the onions. Sauté them gently with the lid on until the onion is transparent but not discolored. Mash the onions with a fork, add the arrowroot diluted in water, and the sea salt, bring the mixture to a boil and simmer for five minutes. Turn into a small dish to set. The "butter" will keep for several days if refrigerated.

(80) **Peanut "Butter"**

1 lb. shelled peanuts
Preheat oven to 350°F.
½ tsp. sea salt
several tablespoons oil

Spread the peanuts out on a baking sheet. Roast at 350°F. for fifteen minutes, stirring occasionally to ensure uniform toasting. Set the blender at "grind" and crush a few nuts at a time, adding oil gradually to get a smooth paste. Add the sea salt and mix well. Store the "butter" in clean screw topped glass jars. This "butter" keeps fairly well without refrigerating if no flavoring or water is added.

(81) **Sesame "Butter"**

1 lb. hulled sesame seeds
½ tsp. crushed sea salt
oil as required

Spread the sesame seeds out on a baking tin to roast at 350°F. for fifteen minutes, stirring occasionally to color uniformly to a light gold. Put a handful at a time into the blender and add oil gradually to make a smooth paste. When all are liquidized stir in the crushed sea salt and mix well. Keep chilled in a glass dish.

CREAM, CUSTARD AND CHEESE SUBSTITUTES

(83) **Magic Cream**

1 egg, lightly poached in 1 cup water (or 1 raw egg yolk)
2 tbs. oil
1 to 2 tbs. honey
scraped vanilla bean or lemon juice to taste

Liquidize all ingredients together in a blender until a smooth cream is produced. If it is too thick add a little more water and whisk in.

(N.B. Some bottles of oil will not thicken. Try refrigerating the mixture. If not successful add oil slowly through the open top to the egg and honey, then add to this the first thin mixture and keep on liquidizing. This should thicken to cream. Use in moderation only.)

(85) **Mock Cream (2)**

1 cup chilled concentrated soya milk (72)
1 tsp. honey
scant pinch of sea salt
½ tsp. lemon juice
1 tbs. oil

Liquidize the first four ingredients in the blender until thoroughly mixed. Add the oil gradually and continue liquidizing until all the oil is absorbed. Chill.

(86) **Magic Custard (1)**

1 orange peeled, quartered and seeded
juice of ½ lemon
1 cooking apple, peeled, cored and quartered
2 tbs. soya flour
1 to 2 tbs. honey
grating of ginger root

Place all the ingredients in the blender and blend until very smooth. If the mixture is too thick add a little lemon juice, if too thin add a little soya flour. Turn the custard into a small pitcher and serve with suitable desserts.

(87) **Magic Custard (2)**

1 orange, peeled, seeded and quartered
1 dessert apple, cored and quartered
juice of ½ lemon
2 tsp. honey
pinch scraped vanilla bean
oil as required

Liquidize all ingredients in a blender except the oil until quite smooth. Add the oil gradually (as for mayonnaise) until the custard is of the desired consistency. Chill and serve in a pitcher with suitable desserts or in individual custard cups garnished with chopped nuts.

(88) **Nut "Cheese"**

6 tbs. nut "butter"
6 tbs. soya flour (or more as required)
good pinch of turmeric powder

Melt the nut "butter" gently in a pan. Stir in the soya flour gradually to make a thick paste, then stir in the turmeric (for its cosmetic value). Press the mixture into a small round glass dish or cup and chill until the "cheese" has hardened. Plunge the dish into hot water for a few seconds to unmold. It should be possible to cut the "cheese" in slices and grate it.

(89) **Soya "Cheese"**

1 cup full fat soya flour
1 cup cold water
2 cups boiling water
juice of 2 lemons
½ tsp. sea salt
chopped chives, parsley, celery seeds, etc. as desired

Make a smooth paste of the soya flour and cold water. Add to the boiling water and cook for five minutes. Add the lemon juice. Remove and set aside to cool. When it curdles, strain through a cheese cloth spread over a colander. Put the "cheese" into a bowl and season with plenty of the desired seasoning. Chill before serving on small potato cakes (205) or potato bread (28).

Chapter 7

DESSERTS

Fruit is the very best dessert for anyone anywhere. All fruits except quinces are best eaten ripe and raw.

Bowls of fresh fruit in season, mixed to provide contrasts of color and shape, mixed fruit salads, cut melons, avocados, grapefruit and so on, carefully garnished on attractive dishes, please both the eye and the taste buds and are full of health-giving natural sweetness. Even a wooden bowl of dried fruits and nuts can look very appealing, especially if the fruits are home-dried.

Using fresh fruit not only saves time but provides food that no sort of treatment can equal, for the vitamins remain unharmed by the addition of sugar or the effects of cooking.

Whenever fruit is cooked it should never be stewed but dropped into a minimum of boiling water, with no sugar added, and cooked as quickly and lightly as possible. A few raisins may be added to sweeten it or you may use a little honey diluted with water. Serve the honey in a small pitcher so that it can be poured out.

Home-canned fruit is not, of course, raw but is a useful way of preserving surplus summer fruit for use in winter. If the fruit is put up as soon as it is picked, the temperature of the water kept below boiling point and no sugar added, very little vitamin C is lost. The vitamin is further preserved by storing the fruit in the dark.

Commercially canned fruits are, unfortunately, heavily sweetened with white sugar and the higher the price the higher the sugar content. However, it is possible to buy water-packed unsweetened canned fruit. Read labels. Enquire at your health food store.

The following recipes are concessions to human frailty and perhaps limited budgets.

(90) **Apple Cream**

¾ cup apple juice
2 egg yolks (reserve the whites for batter or droppies)
2 tbs. honey
1 tbs. lemon juice

Mix all the ingredients thoroughly in a bowl. Stand the bowl in a pan of warm water and beat the contents with a rotary beater until creamy. If the cream becomes too thick add a little more lemon juice. Chill. Serve in individual glasses.

(92) **Apple Pudding** (baked)

4 cooking apples
1 lemon
2 tbs. water
2 eggs
1½ tbs. oil
2 tbs. honey

Preheat oven to 325°F.
Peel and core the apples carefully and cut them into small pieces. Drop them into a pan with the juice and grated rind (yellow only) of the lemon and two tablespoonfuls of boiling water. Simmer until soft. Beat the egg well and mix it with the honey and oil. Blend the mixture well with the apple and turn them into an oiled glass pie plate standing in a baking dish half filled with water. Bake at 325°F. for about thirty minutes or until the pudding is set firm.

(93) **Arrowroot Mold** (cold)

4 heaped tbs. arrowroot
1½ pints soya milk (73)
2 tbs. honey
¼ inch vanilla bean
1 tsp. raw beet juice

Mix the arrowroot smoothly with a little of the cold soya milk in a bowl. Bring the rest of the milk and vanilla bean to boiling point, pour it over the arrowroot paste after removing vanilla, and stir well. Add the honey and beet juice. Return the mixture to the pan and simmer gently for a few minutes. Pour into a wetted mold and chill. Turn out and serve with puréed fruit or Magic Cream (83).

(94) **Arrowroot Pudding** (baked)

1 tbs. arrowroot
¾ pint soya milk (73)
1 to 2 tbs. honey
2 egg yolks, beaten
2 egg whites, beaten
pinch of sea salt
scraped vanilla bean

Preheat oven to 325°F.

Mix the arrowroot smoothly with a little soya milk. Boil the rest of the milk and add it to the arrowroot paste, stirring all the time. Return the mixture to the pan and simmer gently until it thickens, then cool slightly. Add the honey and the well beaten egg yolks and stir at a lower heat for a few minutes then fold in the egg whites. Pour into an oiled glass pie plate and bake at 325°F. for about thirty minutes or until set.

(95) **Arrowroot Soufflé**

2 tbs. arrowroot
1 pint soya milk (73)
2 tbs. honey
grated ginger root or nutmeg
½ bay leaf
pinch of salt
4 eggs, separated

Preheat oven to 325°F.

Mix the arrowroot smoothly with a little of the cold milk, bring the rest of the milk to a boil and pour over the paste, stirring well. Return the mixture to the pan, add the honey, desired flavoring, half bay leaf and a pinch of salt and stir. Continue cooking the mixture until it leaves the sides of the pan. Remove the bay leaf, cool slightly and beat in each yolk separately. Then fold in the stiffly beaten whites. Pour into an oiled glass pie plate and bake gently at 325°F. for about twenty to twenty-five minutes.

(96) **Baked Custard**

1 tbs. honey
2 eggs
1 pint soya milk (73)
grating of lemon rind

Preheat oven to 300°F.

Beat the eggs and honey together well and add the soya milk and lemon rind. Turn into an oiled baking dish and let stand it in water. Bake at 300°F. until set firm and brown.

(97) **Banana Custard**

4 bananas
juice of 1 lemon
2 tbs. honey
2 eggs, separated
¾ pint soya milk (73)

Preheat oven to 325°F.

Peel the bananas and cut them into one-inch pieces. Lay the pieces in an oven dish and sprinkle with lemon juice and honey. Set aside for thirty minutes. Beat the egg yolks and mix in the soya milk. Beat the whites stiffly, fold them into the mixture and bake at 325°F. for about forty-five minutes or until set.

(98) **Berry Mousse**

2 cups fruit purée (fresh or bottled bilberries, black, red or white currants, loganberries, raspberries, or any other soft fruit available)
1 tsp. agar-agar dissolved in 2 tbs. boiling water and boiled for 1 minute
1 cup Magic cream (83)

Chill the fruit purée. Add the agar-agar solution and fold in the Magic cream. Put into individual serving glasses, garnish with a couple of whole berries and chill again.

(99) **Black Currant and Date Whip**

1 cup hot water
½ cup chopped dates
2 cups cooked or canned blackcurrants

Put the hot water into a blender and add the dates gradually, followed by the blackcurrants, liquidizing between each addition until smooth (stop and start as needed replacing the top each time). Scrape out with a spatula into serving glasses. Chill. Garnish with a dab of Magic cream (83) before serving.

(100) **Caramel Custard**

Ingredients as for baked custard (96)
1 tbs. honey

Prepare custard as for "baked custard" but before turning it into the oven dish make caramel as follows:
Heat the honey gently in a small pan until the color starts to change. Pour it into an oiled dish and turn to coat the bottom and sides. Leave it to cool a little and then pour on the custard mixture and bake. Cool. Turn out onto a dish. Serve hot or cold.

(101) **Chestnut Cream**

1 cup chestnuts
2 tbs. honey
1 cup soya milk (73)
grated lemon rind

Make a diagonal cross on the flat side of each chestnut and boil them until they are tender on piercing. Peel them. Cook them in the top of a double boiler with the honey, soya milk and lemon rind until tender. Liquidize in a blender or rub through a sieve. Heap up in individual glasses, chill and serve garnished with slivered almonds.

(102) **Chestnut Puree**

2 cups chestnuts
2 cups soya milk (73)
⅛ tsp. scraped vanilla bean pulp
4 tbs. honey

Prepare boiled chestnuts as above. Remove the shells and skin. Cover the kernels with the soya milk, add the vanilla and cook until tender. Add the vanilla and honey to make a moist mixture. Press the mixture through a sieve into individual glasses and garnish with pieces of nuts or raisins.

(103) **Cinnamon Custard** (for special occasions)

3 cups soya milk (73)
½ cup pitted dates
2 egg yolks, beaten
sprinkle of cinnamon or grated nutmeg

Place the milk and dates in the blender and liquidize. Pour

into a bowl set in a pan of boiling water. Stir in the egg yolks and continue stirring until the custard thickens. Pour it into serving glasses and chill. Sprinkle with cinnamon or nutmeg before serving.

(104) **Coconut Pudding**

2 beaten eggs
1 cup soya milk (73)
1 cup finely chopped raisins
1 cup shredded coconut
grated rind of 1 orange or lemon

Preheat oven to 325°F.
Thoroughly mix all the ingredients. Turn them into an oiled glass pie plate and set it in a shallow dish of water. Bake at 325°F. until set. Serve hot or cold with Magic cream (83).

(105) **Coconut Baked Pudding**

3 cups soya milk (73)
1 cup honey
2 tbs. molasses
½ cup shredded coconut
1½ tbs. tapioca
2½ tbs. potato flour
½ tsp. sea salt
1 tsp. lemon juice or the grated rind of 1 lemon

Preheat oven to 350°F.
Bring the milk to a boil, mix all the rest of the ingredients and stir into the milk. Cook the mixture in a double saucepan or a bowl standing in a pan of hot water until it thickens slightly. Turn it into an oiled baking dish, cover and bake at 350°F. for one-and-one-half hours. Remove the cover and continue cooking for another 30 minutes to brown the surface. Serve hot with Magic cream (83).

(106) **Festive Pudding** (with acknowledgement to Doris Grant)

2 beaten egg yolks
1 cup coconut meal
2 cups seeded minced muscatel raisins
½ cup chopped monukka raisins
½ cup chopped dried bananas
½ cup whole monukka raisins
½ cup chopped walnuts
grated lemon rind
lemon juice to moisten

Mix all ingredients to a stiff consistency, thinning with lemon juice as necessary. Steam for one hour in an oiled bowl. Serve hot with Magic cream. (83).

(107) Dried Fruit Steamed Pudding

2 cups raisins
1 cup pitted and chopped dates
2 tbs. soya flour
4 tbs. grated raw potato
4 tbs. dried coconut
2 well beaten eggs
juice of ½ lemon

Mix all the ingredients well in a large bowl. Steam in an oiled, covered bowl for two hours. Turn out and serve.

(108) Fruit Froth

2 cups chopped apples, guavas, berries or any other suitable raw fruit
a grating of lemon rind
honey to taste
2 egg whites, stiffly beaten

(N.B. Raw egg white steals biotin, but this method cooks it lightly.) Liquidize in a blender or sieve the chopped fruit. Put it in a pan and heat to boiling point. Cool slightly and fold in the egg whites, grated lemon rind, and honey to taste. Cool gradually. Pile into individual dessert dishes and top with whole berries or small segments of fruit.

(109) Instant Lemon Pudding

1 cup warm water
3 tbs. agar-agar
2 lightly boiled eggs
2 tbs. honey
1 to 2 tsp. lemon juice
½ cup oil
a few blanched almonds

Place the water and agar-agar in the blender and switch on until the agar has dissolved and the liquid is foaming. Add the eggs, honey and lemon juice and liquidize again. Finally add the oil and liquidize until the mixture thickens. Pour into a wetted mold and chill before unmolding. Garnish with sliced blanched almonds.

(110) **Mincemeat**

⅓ cup oil
1 cup seeded and chopped raisins
½ cup honey
1 cup raisins
grated rind and juice of 1 lemon
½ tsp. each nutmeg and cinnamon or 1 tsp. mixed spice
4 tbs. finely chopped cooking apples

Mix all ingredients together thoroughly in a bowl and press the mixture into a jar. Cover closely and keep refrigerated. Eat from dessert dishes without pastry at Christmas time.

(111) **Molasses Mold** (for occasional use only)

½ cup molasses
1 well-beaten egg yolk
1 cup Magic cream (83)

Heat the molasses to boiling point and pour over the egg yolk in a bowl standing in hot water in a pan. Beat constantly and continue cooking until thickened. Cool and beat in the Magic cream. Turn the mixture into a wetted mold and chill it. Unmold and surround with lemon-flavored apple purée.

(112) **Orange and Apple Whip**

1 cup orange quarters (seeded)
½ cup water
pinch of sea salt
2 large cooking apples, cored and chopped
5 dates, pitted

Put the orange quarters into a blender with the water and salt and turn on. Gradually add the chopped apple and dates. Spoon into glass dishes and garnish with dabs of Magic cream (83) or pieces of orange.

(113) **Orange Pudding**

2 separated eggs
¼ cup honey
4 oz. soya flour
2 oz. potato flour
Preheat oven to 350°F.
½ cup soya milk
¾ cup orange juice
1 tbs. lemon juice
grated rind of 1 lemon
1½ tbs. oil

Beat the egg yolks and fold in the honey. Add the soya flour and potato flour and the soya milk alternately. Then add the juices, rind and oil. Beat the egg whites until stiff then fold in. Turn the mixture into an oiled glass pie plate and set it in a pan of warm water. Bake at 350°F. for about forty-five minutes. When ready the pudding should be crisp on top and more liquid underneath. Try eating it cold as a change from hot.

(114) **Pancakes** (baked)

½ pint soya milk (73)
1 tbs. oil
2 eggs
2 tbs. potato flour
bay leaf or grated lemon rind
4 tbs. apricot spread (273) or mock chocolate spread (277)

Preheat oven to 425°F.

Heat the soya milk. Beat the oil and honey until smooth, beat in the eggs and stir in the potato flour lightly. Now add the warm soya milk, which will slightly curdle the mixture. Add bay leaf or lemon rind. Beat well then cover and put aside for about one hour. Have ready six large oiled oven-proof saucers. Put an equal amount of batter in each and bake at 425° F. for about ten minutes or until the batter rises and then decrease to 350° F. for another ten minutes. Cover the tops of five pancakes with warmed spread, place them one on the other, then place the plain one on top, dredge with a little dried coconut and cut into wedges. Serve at once.

(115) **Prune Whip**

1½ cups apple juice
2 tbs. lemon juice
pinch of sea salt
¾ cup soaked pitted prunes
¾ cup diced dates
4 blanched almonds
½ tsp. almond butter (see pp. 41-42) (optional)

Pour the apple juice into a blender with the lemon juice and a pinch of salt. Turn on and add the rest of the ingredients gradually. Blend until smooth. Scrape out the whip with a spatula into dessert dishes and chill. Top with chopped or halved almonds before serving.

(116) **Pumpkin Custard**

1½ cups pumpkin pulp
3 eggs
1½ cups soya flour
pinch of sea salt
3 tbs. honey (less if pumpkin is extra sweet)
cinnamon for sprinkling

Preheat oven to 300°F.
Liquidize all the ingredients in a blender except the cinnamon. Pour the mixture into an oiled glass pie plate or individual dishes and sprinkle with cinnamon. Stand the pie plate in a pan of water and bake at 300°F. for about forty minutes until firm. (A straw inserted into the custard should come out clean.) Serve hot or cold.

(117) **Pumpkin Puree**

Remove the seeds and membranes from a large slice of pumpkin and cut it up into small wedges. Set the wedges on a rack over a little boiling water in a pan and cover. Simmer for about fifteen minutes until tender. Reserve the water for gravy, stew or soup. Remove the skin and purée the flesh smoothly, adding a little honey to sweeten. Pile into individual glasses and garnish with a sprinkle of cinnamon, raisins or chopped nuts as desired. Chill and serve with Magic cream (83).

(118) **Pumpkin Spicy Pudding**

2 cups mashed cooked pumpkin
¼ to ½ cup honey (less if pumpkin is extra sweet)
½ cup soya milk (73)
2 eggs
generous grating of nutmeg
1 tbs. (scant) oil

Preheat oven to 350°F.
Remove the seeds and membranes of the pumpkin and cut it into wedges. Steam the wedges for about fifteen to twenty minutes until tender. Cool, peel, drain and mash

them in a bowl until smooth. Add the honey, soya milk and eggs, beating lightly. Turn the mixture into an oiled pie plate and smooth it with the back of a fork. Grate the nutmeg generously over the surface and sprinkle with oil. Bake at 350°F. for about thirty minutes but do not overbrown

(119) **Raisin Fool**

½ cup seedless raisins
4 tbs. water
2 cooking apples
4 almonds or cinnamon to sprinkle

Soak the raisins in water overnight or for forty-eight hours until tender and swollen. Wash, wipe, quarter and core the apples (and peel them if they have not been organically grown). Liquidize the apples with the raisins and the soaking water in a blender. Scrape the fool into four dessert dishes. Blanch the almonds, halve them and use them to garnish the fool, or sprinkle it with cinnamon powder. (Pitted, cooked Bing cherries, gooseberries, plums or rhubarb, etc., can be used in place of apples.)

(120) **Raisin Syrup**

1 cup seedless raisins
3 cups water

Cook the raisins in water until reduced to one and a half cups (This is nearly equal to one cup of sugar). Transfer to the blender, liquidize and strain through a sieve. (Do not discard the pulp but use it to sweeten other foods or serve on its own with Magic cream (83). Serve the liquid as a sauce or use it for sweetening in other recipes, or fruit salads.

(121) **Soya Crumble**

½ tsp. sea salt
8 tbs. soya flour
4 tbs. sunflower oil
grated rind of ½ lemon
cold water as required

Preheat oven to 350°F.

Stir the crushed sea salt into the soya flour. Rub in the oil with the fingers, add the lemon rind and just enough cold water to hold the dough together, but let it stay crumbly.

Press into a nine-inch baking pan and bake at 350°F. for fifteen minutes. When chilled, crumble over apple purée, or any other cooked fruit.

(122) **Soya Pancakes**

3 eggs
pinch of sea salt
4 tbs. soya flour
½ pint hot water

Liquidize the eggs, salt and soya flour until smooth and thick. Put into a bowl and stir in enough hot water to make a thin batter. Transfer to a pitcher. Brush a hot pan with oil and pour in enough batter to make a thin pancake. Brown on both sides and fold in two. Set the cooked pancakes aside on a hot plate until all are cooked. Serve with mixed lemon juice and honey.

(123) **Sweet Pancakes**

½ cup warm water
1 tbs. honey or molasses
1½ tsp. dried baking yeast
1 cup soya milk (73)
2 tbs. oil
1 cup potato flour
pinch of sea salt

Pour the water onto the honey in a bowl and stir. Sprinkle the yeast on top and leave in a warm place to froth up. Add the soya milk and oil then fold in the potato flour and salt. Set aside for several hours. Pour three tablespoonfuls of batter for each pancake, about five inches across, onto a moderately hot griddle or frying pan. Cook slowly and turn to brown both sides. Stack on a dish in a warm oven and serve at once with apple purée or other puréed fruit.

(124) **Sweet Potato Fruit Tartlets**

2 cups shredded sweet potato
2 tbs. oil
any variety of fruit purée

Preheat oven to 425°F.

Scrub the sweet potato and peel it. Shred it finely on a stainless steel grater and sauté in the oil pre-heated in a pan but do not brown. Press the cooked potatoes firmly onto the bottom and sides of oiled patty pans and bake for about ten minutes in a hot oven (425°F). Cool and serve filled with a purée of any fruit available.

(125) **Zabaglione** (without alcohol)

3 egg yolks
3 tbs. honey
3 tbs. apple juice

Beat together the yolks and honey in a bowl until pale and fluffy. Put into the top of a double boiler (or stand the bowl in a pan of hot water), add the slightly warmed apple juice and beat over a good heat for five minutes until the mixture is like whipped cream. Remove from the heat and continue beating for two minutes more. Pour into glasses and serve hot or chilled.

Chapter 8

FISH

At one time fish could be regarded as a relatively cheap source of protein, providing about the same amount as an equivalent quantity of meat. Unfortunately the difference in price between fish and meat has, over the last few years, become much less, but fish still has the advantages of being easily digestible and quickly cooked using simple recipes. Fish is good quality protein and also a good source of unsaturated fats. Ocean fish also offer minerals, trace minerals such as iodine, and a high content of B complex vitamins.

Fish livers, where vitamins A and D are chiefly stored are, unfortunately, seldom eaten.

Another advantage of fish is that, not yet having been farmed extensively, they are free from the residues of hormones, antibiotics and all the other artificial aids to modern animal husbandry. Fish are clearly a good buy and should be served at least once or twice a week either at breakfast or main meals. A common cause of complaint from the kitchen are the smells that accompany fish. These can be obviated by keeping cooking temperatures low and fishy smells can be removed from the hands by washing with a little vinegar. If possible use only fresh fish. Frozen fish should be allowed to thaw slowly at room temperature, then cooked at once. To wash fresh fish, dip it in a shallow dish of salted water containing about one teaspoonful of salt to a pint of water. This will help to preserve the flavor. Do not, however, add salt to the fish before cooking as this will draw out the flavor and nutritional value. Fish juices contain the same amount of salt as the ocean and by making the washing water approximately the same strength they remain unaffected.

Since you must not use flour, crumbs or batter, don't attempt to brown fish without the aid of paprika or oil. Generous sprinkling with paprika before cooking will achieve a rich brown.

(126) **Baked Stuffed Herrings**

1 shallot or small onion
4 sprigs parsley
1 cup grated raw potato
1 tbs. oil
¼ tsp. sea salt
1 well-beaten egg
4 herrings

Preheat oven to 375°F.

Chop the onion and parsley finely and mix with the grated potato, oil and salt. Bind with the beaten egg. Split the herrings and remove the backbone and as many small bones as possible. Spread a quarter of the mixture on each open herring. Fold over and secure with strong thread. Place in an oiled casserole and bake at 375°F. for ten minutes covered, then uncovered for about ten minutes longer.

(127) **Curried Fish** (without curry powder)

½ coconut
1 cup boiling soya milk (73)
1 large cooking apple
1 large onion
2 tbs. oil
1 lb. steamed flaked fish
1 crushed bay leaf
1 tsp. ground ginger
1 cup water
1 small chili pepper
1 outer onion skin
sprinkle of turmeric powder
sea salt to taste

Prepare the coconut milk one hour before the meal as follows. Grate the coconut into a bowl, pour the boiling soya milk over it, cover and set aside. Wash and core the apple and peel the onion, reserving a large piece of clean outer skin. Chop the apple and onion finely. Heat the oil in a pan and put in the fish, onion, apple and bay leaf. Sauté gently until the onion is brown. Mix together the ground ginger, water, chili and onion skin and add to the other ingredients. Simmer gently for about twenty minutes. Remove the chili and onion skin. Strain off the milk from the grated coconut, sprinkle in the turmeric powder and stir to color a good yellow and add to the fish mixture. Taste for salt. Serve ringed by mashed potato.

(128) **Fish Baked with Lemon**

1 large lemon
1 cup water
1 tbs. oil
1 small lemon
1 clove garlic (optional)
2 tsp. mashed potato
4 fillets or white fish steaks

Preheat oven to 350°F.

Squeeze and strain the juice from the large lemon and add to a cupful of water in a small pan. Grate in the rind. Add half the oil and bring slowly to a boil. Add the skin and finely chopped pulp of the small lemon and, if desired, the pulped garlic clove. Dissolve the mashed potato in enough water to make a thin paste and pour it into the boiling mixture in the pan. Stir the mixture until it thickens and clears. Add the second half of the oil, pour the sauce over the fish pieces arranged in an oiled dish, cover with parchment paper and bake at 350°F. for about twenty minutes.

(129) **Fish Baked with Onion**

1 tbs. oil
4 fish fillets or steaks
1 small onion, grated
sprinkle of paprika

Preheat oven to 375°F.

Brush an oven dish with oil and lay the fish in it, adding the grated onion. Brush with the rest of the oil and bake at 375°F. for about fifteen minutes more or less, according to the thickness of the fish. Sprinkle with paprika and salt, if desired, before serving.

(130) **Fish Omelets**

2 tbs. sunflower oil
3 tbs. chopped parsley
1 cup fresh shrimp, cooked and shelled
4 egg whites
1 tbs. soy flour
1 scant tbs. lemon juice

Sauté the parsley gently in the heated oil. Add the shrimps and cook for another minute. Crack the egg whites into a bowl and set the yolks aside for use in another recipe. Do not beat the whites, but when the parsley is still crisp but tender stir the contents of the pan gently into the bowl with the whites. Stir well then drop by small cupfuls into the oiled pan to make small omelets. Mix together the soya flour and lemon juice and pour them into the pan after removing the omelets. Heat the sauce, pour it over the omelets and serve.

(131) **Fish Salad**

4 pieces cold steamed fish
1 tbs. lemon juice
2 tbs. finely chopped raisins
½ cup home-made mayonnaise (223, 224, 225)
1 lettuce
1 sweet red pepper (optional)

Flake the fish. Mix the lemon juice and raisins well, add them to the fish and toss in the mayonnaise to coat evenly. Chill. Wash the lettuce rapidly and whirl it dry. Set the leaves out on a glass dish and pile the fish in the center to serve. Garnish with sweet pepper cut into strips.

(132) **Fried Fish** (without batter or breadcrumbs)

4 fish steaks
paprika
2 tbs. oil

Wash the steaks, dry them well and dredge with paprika. Heat the oil in a pan and fry the steaks over a moderate heat until brown. Do not cover. Turn with a spatula to brown the other side. Serve with lemon wedges or lemon sauce (244).

(133) **Fried Smelts**

1 lb. smelts
paprika for dredging
1 tbs. oil
sprinkle of sea salt
4 lemon wedges

Wash the fish and dry it well. Leave on the heads and tails. Dredge with paprika. Heat a large pan, brush with oil, and arrange the smelts either head and tail alternately or with the heads at the edge and the tails in the center. Cook until half the thickness of the fish looks opaque, then turn with a spatula carefully and cook the other side until nicely brown and crisp. Sprinkle with sea salt and serve at once with lemon wedges, on a round dish.

(134) **Greek Fish Salad**

2 tbs. chopped onion
2 tbs. chopped parsley
½ bay leaf
pinch of sea salt
5 tbs. oil
juice of 1 lemon
1 lb. white fish, steamed and chilled
1 head lettuce
celery for garnish

Liquidize the onion, parsley, bay leaf and salt with the oil and lemon juice. Dice the fish neatly and set it in the middle of a dish fringed by lettuce leaves. Pour the dressing over it and chill. Serve garnished with celery fingers.

(135) **Broiled Fish**

4 fish fillets (under 1½ in. thick
oil to brush
paprika to brown
no salt

Preheat broiler.

Set the unskinned fillets on a wire rack in the broiling pan. Brush with oil and sprinkle thoroughly with paprika. With gas set the rack about one inch, and with electricity set it about five inches from the heat. Keep the heat low and leave the oven door open. Turn with a spatula after about four to five minutes. Allow the same time for the other side. Garnish with chopped chives or parsley.

(136) Broiled Roe

1 lb. hard roe in membrane
a little oil

Preheat broiler.
Brush the roe with oil. Lay it on the broiling pan to cook under a low heat for twenty minutes. Do not turn. Serve with a wedge of lemon and chopped chives or parsley.

(137) Broiled Shrimps

1 to 2 pints unshelled, full size shrimp
½ cup oil
½ bay leaf
½ tsp. sea salt
2 tbs. chopped parsley

Preheat broiler.
Shell the shrimps and leave them to marinate in the other ingredients combined in a covered container in the refrigerator overnight. Transfer both the shrimps and the marinade to a shallow baking dish and broil under a brisk heat for about six minutes. Serve with a tossed green salad and mashed potato sprinkled with paprika.

(138) Herrings in Crisps

4 whole herrings
1 lightly beaten egg
2 tbs. oil
1 packet crushed potato chips (guaranteed grain- or gluten-free)

Cut off the heads and tails of the herrings and gut them. Run the thumb down under the backbone and lift it out with the rest of the bones. Flatten each fish, dip it in the beaten egg and roll it in crushed potato chips. Sauté the fish in heated oil until crisp, then turn to brown the other side. Serve garnished with parsley.

(139) Kipper Cakes

1 lb. kipper or smoked mackerel fillets
4 mashed medium-sized potatoes
2 chopped hard boiled eggs
chopped parsley
1 raw egg, beaten
2 tbs. oil
a little lentil, pea, potato or soya flour for coating

Stand the fillets in a bowl, pour boiling water over them

and leave for five minutes. Skin and flake the fish off the bones and mix thoroughly with the potato, hard-boiled eggs and parsley. Pat flat and cut out with a wine glass into small circles. Dip in beaten egg, toss in a paper bag holding the selected flour and sauté in heated oil. Serve hot.

(140) **Lobster Creams**

1 lobster
½ tsp. anchovy fillets
1 tbs. lemon juice
1 sprig tarragon, finely chopped
¼ cup soya flour
1 large lettuce

Boil the lobster, cool and flake it, removing and reserving the roe. Then pound it with the anchovy, lemon juice, tarragon and soya flour and fill the mixture into small ramekin cases. Scatter lobster coral (roe) on top and garnish with tiny parsley sprigs. Serve in the cases on a bed of lettuce.

(141) **Fish and Onion Pie**

1 lb. white fish fillets
2 tbs. chopped parsley
½ cup finely chopped onion
sea salt to taste
½ cup soya milk (73)
1½ tbs. oil
1 cup mashed potato

Preheat oven to 375°F.
Wash the fillets and cut them in pieces. Lay a few pieces in an oiled pie plate. Sprinkle with chopped parsley and onion and a little salt. Continue with similar layers until all are used. Add the soya milk. Add nearly all the oil to the potato, spread the potato over the fish and ripple the surface with the back of a fork. Sprinkle with the remainder of the oil and bake for about twenty minutes at 375°F.

(142) **Quick Fish Dish**

2 large onions
2 tbs. oil
4 medium fillets of any white fish, scaled but not skinned
sprinkle of paprika

Sauté the chopped onion in the heated oil until transparent

only. Dice the fish into one-inch cubes and scatter them over the onion. Cook gently with the lid on for about five minutes until all pinkness has vanished. Sprinkle with paprika and serve at once with mashed potato and watercress.

(143) **Salmon Omelet**

1 cup canned salmon
1 small onion
2 tsp. lemon juice
2 tsp. finely chopped parsley
3 separated eggs
1 tbs. oil

Mash the salmon well and add the finely grated raw onion with the lemon juice and parsley. Beat the egg whites until they form stiff peaks and fold into the well beaten yolks. Heat the oil in a frying pan and pour in the eggs. Meanwhile warm up the salmon and when the underside of the omelet is firm, lay the salmon along one side of the upper surface. Fold over the omelet to cover the fish, turn once or twice and serve at once.

(144) **Scallop Stuffed Potatoes**

4 scallops
4 large old potatoes
2 tbs. oil plus extra for brushing potatoes
2 tsp. finely chopped onion
dash of lemon juice

Preheat oven to 400°F.

Put the scallops in a pan in just enough boiling water to cover and simmer gently for about twelve minutes. Drain and set the broth aside. Brush the potatoes all over with oil, pierce with a fork and bake at 400°F. for about one hour or until tender. Scoop out the pulp and mix with the oil, broth, chopped onion and lemon juice. Put one scallop in each cavity and pour the mixture over them. Reheat if necessary before serving.

(145) **Scrambled Fish**

4 eggs
2 tbs. water
sea salt to taste
¼ lb. flaked fish (fresh or leftovers)
2 tbs. oil

Beat the eggs and water just enough to mix the white and yolk, adding salt as desired, and add the flaked fish. Heat the oil in a pan, turn in the mixture and stir gently over a very low heat until the mixture thickens. Serve with jacket potatoes and a green vegetable.

(146) **Spicy Herrings**

4 herrings
2 tbs. oil
½ cup lemon juice
¾ tsp. sea salt
¼ tsp. ground ginger
½ tsp. honey

Preheat oven to 400°F.
Clean and split the fish, removing the backbone and small bones. Mix together all the other ingredients and pour them over the fish. Cover and bake at 400°F. for about twenty-five minutes. Eat hot or cold.

(147) **Steamed Fish**

4 fillets or slices of fish
½ tsp. oil
1 tsp. lemon juice
sprinkle of paprika
sprinkle of sea salt

Brush the oil over a soup or other deep plate. Lay the fish on it, sprinkle with salt, paprika and lemon juice and cover with parchment paper. Set the plate over a large pan of boiling water and cover with a similar plate or a pot cover. Keep the water boiling hard and cook for about fifteen minutes or until tender.

Chapter 9

ICES

You or your patient may not eat commercial ices because they all contain forbidden grain or milk products but that is no reason to entirely deny these youthful delights. They can be made at home with milk-free, grain-free ingredients, as in the following recipes.

(148) **Basic Ice Cream**

1 pint soya milk (73)
2 tbs. honey
2 whole eggs
2 egg yolks
¼ inch vanilla bean

Warm half a pint of soya milk and the honey in a pan. Beat the eggs and yolks well in a bowl. Place the bowl in a pan of hot water and add the milk and honey mixture. Add the vanilla or other desired flavoring and cook gently, stirring continuously until the mixture thickens. Cool and add the remaining half pint of soya milk. Freeze. After about ninety minutes, when crystals have formed around the edges, turn the mixture into a bowl and beat well. Alternatively leave the mixture in the tray and beat it, drawing it in from the sides to the center. Return the tray to the freezer until the ice is set to the desired consistency. Any fruit or chopped nuts can be folded in before the final freezing.

(149) **Coconut Ice (special)**

1 cup fresh grated or dried coconut
2 cups Magic cream (83)
½ cup raisin syrup (120)

Combine the ingredients and pour them into a freezing tray. Place the tray in the refrigerator and when the sides have set remove the mixture to a bowl and beat well with a rotary beater or fork. Return the mixture to the refrigerator to freeze. Garnish with ground nuts or as desired.

(150) **Fruit Ice Cream** (inexpensive)

1 cup fruit purée
2 tsp. lemon juice
1 tbs. honey (if purée is unsweetened)

Purée any fresh or canned fruit by rubbing it through a sieve or by using a blender. Stir the purée into Basic Ice Cream (148) before freezing.

(151) **Ice Cream** (inexpensive)

1 scant tbs. agar-agar
2 tbs. hot water
1 pint soya milk (73)
4 to 6 tbs. honey
1 egg
scraped vanilla bean to taste

Dissolve the agar-agar in the hot water. Warm the soya milk and stir in the honey until dissolved. Beat the egg in a bowl and stir in the soya milk mixture and vanilla. Place the bowl in a pan of hot water and heat with continuous stirring until almost boiling. Do not allow to boil or the egg will curdle. Take the pan off the heat, add the agar-agar and stir until dissolved. When cold set the mixture in the freezer. When the edges are set beat with a fork from the sides to the center and leave to set firm again before serving.

(152) **Surprise Ice Pudding (special)**

2 cups thick Magic cream (83)
1 cup diced apple
1 cup quartered tangerines or halved orange quarters

Coat a shallow dish with one cupful of the cream. Freeze. Fill the center of the ice with fruit and cover with the rest of the cream. Freeze thoroughly. Turn out onto a cold dish and garnish with chopped nuts or blanched almond halves.

(153) Water Ices

2 cups soft fruit (fresh, stewed or canned without sugar)
1 cup water
honey to taste (for tart fruit)
lemon juice (for sweet fruit)
chopped nuts to garnish

Liquidize the fruit, water and honey (or lemon juice) in a blender. Turn the mixture into a shallow dish and put the dish into the freezing compartment of the refrigerator. When the sides have set beat the mixture with a fork drawing the sides to the center. Repeat once or twice. Spoon into dessert dishes and garnish with chopped nuts or as desired.

Chapter 10

MEATS

Most cookbooks give plenty of recipes for using expensive cuts but few supply enough recipes for using what are by far the most valuable parts of the beast—the organ meats. Liver, kidney and heart are excellent foods because among meats they are the best source of the vitamin B complex (especially of folic acid, vitamin B12 and pantothenic acid), of minerals and of superior quality proteins. In the United States before World War I liver used to be given only to dogs, drawing the acid comment from a nutritionist that this appeared to be one of the reasons why this country produced over one hundred breeds of splendid dogs but generations of young men suffering from every kind of degenerative disease, as revealed by the recruiting statistics. Those who value their health eat liver or the other organ meats at least once or twice a week. So a great many different ways of serving them are included here.*

Since the price of meat is generally very high, recipes using the cheaper cuts, either as they are or chopped, are also given.

*Unfortunately, since liver and kidney are filters they concentrate the dubious residues from modern farming, and people unable to obtain these meats from suitable sources (i.e. from animals reared on farms that use no pesticides, antibiotics or hormones) may prefer to get their folic acid from the foliage (i.e. leaves) of raw green vegetables and their vitamin B12 from comfrey or a supplement.

(154) **Bacon and Bean Pot** (simple)

1 cup haricot beans*
bouquet garni (1 sprig each parsley, thyme, marjoram)
4 slices of lean bacon**

Preheat oven to 325°F.
Soak the beans in the refrigerator overnight in enough water to cover them. Next day put the beans with the herbs and bacon into an ovenproof jar or cooking pot. Barely cover with cold water, put the lid on the pot and simmer at 300°F. until tender. Serve with a cooked green, leafy vegetable.

(155) **Baked Beans**

2 cups dried beans
2 slices lean bacon
bouquet garni (parsley, thyme, marjoram)
1 large onion, chopped
2 large tomatoes, chopped
1 green pepper, chopped
1 tbs. molasses
sea salt
pepper if desired

Soak the beans overnight in the refrigerator and next day simmer them with the bacon and bouquet garni, barely covered with water, in a tightly sealed oven pot until half cooked. Then remove the herbs and mix in the chopped vegetables with the molasses and seasoning to taste. Halve the bacon rashers, place them on top of the vegetables and finish cooking without the lid.

(156) **Beef and Bean Curry** (without curry powder)

4oz. dried beans (soaked in ½ pint water and left in the refrigerator overnight)
1 good sized onion
2 tbs. oil
½ lb. raw ground beef
1 clove garlic (optional)
1 tsp. tumeric powder
4 tbs. water or stock

Soften the onion in the oil, then stir in the beef, garlic and turmeric powder. Cook, stirring, for about five minutes

*Any dried variety will be good: pea, navy, kidney, turtle, etc.

**All bacon must be nitrite-free and not sugar-cured. Substitute sea salt if not available.

then add the beans, with liquids, stir well, cover and cook gently for up to one hour until tender.

(157) **Beef Cake**

1 finely chopped onion
1 tbs. oil
1 lb. ground beef
1 tbs. chopped parlsey
sea salt to taste
1 sliced cooked carrot
1 egg yolk
1 turnip or sweet potato, cooked and mashed

Preheat oven to 375°F.

Toss the onion in hot oil until tender but not brown. Add the beef and cook for three minutes, then add the parsley and season with salt. Oil a casserole and cover the base with rows of sliced carrot. Spread half the meat mixture in a layer over this. Beat the egg yolk into the mashed turnip or sweet potato and spread the mixture in a layer over the meat. Then cover with the rest of the meat in a layer. Cover and bake in a fairly hot oven (375°) for fifteen minutes. Cool slightly, turn out onto a warm dish and serve with a cooked green vegetable or a salad.

(158) **Beef Chop Suey** (without rice)

3 tbs. oil
3 medium-sized onions, chopped
4 large stalks celery, sliced
¾ lb. ground beef
1 pint mung bean sprouts (optional)
1 to 2 tbs. dark molasses
2 tbs. soya flour
2 tbs. cold water
½ cup sliced mushrooms
2 cups mashed potato

Heat the oil in a pan and sauté the onions until tender. Add the celery and cook for two minutes longer, then add the beef and cook over a high heat for two minutes. Remove the beef and set aside. Add the mung bean sprouts and enough water to cover. Bring to a boil and simmer, covered, for fifteen minutes. Combine the molasses, soya flour and water and stir them into the bean sprout mixture. Add the mushrooms and beef, reheat, and serve surrounded by mashed potato with a tossed green salad.

(159) Rollatine of Beef

1 lb. round steak
4 tbs. grated raw potato
1 grated medium carrot
1 grated medium onion
½ tsp. sea salt
1 egg yolk, beaten
soya flour
2 tbs. oil
1 cup vegetable water or water

Beat the meat well, then cut it into thin strips about four inches by three inches. Mix the grated potato, carrot, onion and salt with the beaten egg and add enough soya flour to make a firm paste. Spread a layer of this on each slice of beef then roll it up and tie firmly with coarse thread. Heat the oil in a pan and fry the rolls till lightly brown. Add the vegetable water, cover and simmer gently for one-and-three-quarter to two hours, or until tender, adding more fluid if required. Cut off the thread, arrange the beef with the gravy in the center of a hot dish and ring with emerald potatoes. (285).

(160) Beef and Potato Loaf

2 lb. ground beef
1 cup liquidized or sieved tomato
1 onion, finely chopped
2 cups finely shredded raw potato
1 tbs. chopped parsley
1 finely shredded carrot
2 lightly beaten eggs
1 tsp. sea salt

Preheat oven to 375°F.

Mix all ingredients thoroughly and pack them into an oiled 9in. x 5in. x 3in. loaf pan. Bake at 375°F. for thirty minutes or until done. Turn out and serve hot or cold with cooked greens or a salad.

(161) Braised Pigs' Feet

4 pigs' feet
paprika
2 tbs. oil
½ cup lemon juice
grating of nutmeg
1 tsp. molasses
1 to 2 tsp. sea salt
1 minced garlic clove (optional)
1 to 2 cups fresh or canned tomatoes
a little mashed potato or potato flour to thicken

Ask the butcher to cut the pig's feet in half lengthways. Leave them to soak in the refrigerator for one to two days. Drain and dry them, reserving the liquid. Coat them with paprika and brown in the heated oil in a pan. Cover with the liquid used for soaking and simmer for three hours until tender. Add the rest of the ingredients and simmer for ten minutes more. Serve hot, preferably with beans or peas.

(162) **Headcheese**

½ pig's head	pinch each of marjoram, basil and thyme
2 pig's feet	2 to 3 tsp. sea salt
1 bay leaf	

Since pig's heads are carefully cleaned and chopped at the slaughterhouse they are little work to prepare. Wash the head and feet well, put them in a large pan and cover with cold water. Bring to the boil and simmer for about four hours or until the meat falls off the bones. Cool and set the head in a colander over a plate, and put the broth in a bowl to chill overnight. This will make them easier and less greasy to deal with. Next day remove all the bones carefully and with a large knife cut the tongue, brains, skin and all the meat into neat small cubes. Skim the fat from the broth, then heat the broth gradually in a pan with the salt, bay leaf and herbs, add the jellied meat and bring to a boil. Taste for seasoning. Simmer for about fifteen minutes then turn into one or more bowls or loaf tins and leave to chill until firm. Serve cold, either sliced or cut into wedges, with potato salad and watercress or other green salad.

(163) **Pot Roasted Duck with Orange Sauce**

brush of oil	1 onion
1 duck	sprinkle of sea salt
1 to 2 oranges	

Brush the cooking pot with oil and place the duck in it. Add the juice of the oranges and the diced onion. Cover the pot closely and raise heat to medium. Turn the bird frequently to brown all over; then turn the heat low and leave until tender. The cooking time depends on the size of the bird and can take from one to three hours. Sprinkle lightly with sea salt and remove to a hot serving dish. Thicken the juices with a little mashed potato if desired. Serve with mashed potatoes, brussels sprouts or cabbage. If liked, put a sprig of sage in the body cavity.

(164) Ham★ and Potato Balls
(Nitrite-free and not sugar-cured)

- 3 tbs. oil
- 1 small onion or shallot, finely chopped
- 1 cup finely chopped cooked ham
- 1 cup grated raw potato
- 1 tbs. finely chopped parsley or sage
- pinch of sea salt
- 1 egg
- potato flour for dipping

Brush a pan with one tablespoonful of oil and sauté the onion till lightly brown. Mix together the ham, grated raw potato, parsley and salt. Add them to the onion and stir till hot. Beat the egg and stir it in, continuing to stir until the mixture thickens, then spread it on a plate. When the mixture is cool, shape it into balls or cylinders, roll them in potato flour, spread them out separately on a plate and set them aside. Heat two tablespoonfuls of oil in a pan and sauté the balls till brown. Serve hot, with vegetables.

(165) Ham Ramekins

- 2 eggs, separated
- 2 tbs. water
- 1 cup finely chopped ham
- ½ tsp. mixed dried herbs
- a little paprika

Beat the egg yolks lightly with water. Add the ham and herbs. Fill eight small or four large ramekins about three-quarters full and bake in a moderate oven until set, about ten minutes. Meanwhile beat the egg whites to a peak and pile roughly above the level of the cases. Replace in the oven and bake until the white is crisp and lightly brown. Serve hot with mashed potato and cress or a tossed green salad.

(166) **Hearts with Lemon**

2 tbs. oil
1 small onion, finely chopped
2 calves' hearts or 4 lambs' hearts
2 tbs. potato flour
2 tbs. chopped parsley
juice of ½ lemon
sea salt to taste

Heat the oil in a pan and fry the onion until browned. Slice the hearts thinly across the grain and sauté in the same pan, cooking for about four to five minutes on each side. Mix the potato flour, onion, lemon juice, and fried onion thoroughly. Pour the mixture over the slices and coat them well with it as they re-heat. Serve at once.

(167) **Roast Hearts with Nut Stuffing**

4 large onions
4 lambs' hearts
3 tbs. oil
4 tbs. mashed potato
1 tsp. grated lemon rind
1 tsp. grated lemon rind
pinch of sea salt
2 tbs. chopped filberts or peanuts
1 beaten egg
1 cup vegetable stock or water
parsley

Preheat oven to 400°F.
Peel the onions and steam them on a rack for thirty minutes. Wash the hearts and cut off all fat and tough pieces, including membranes. Make a stuffing by mixing together one tablespoonful of oil with the mashed potato, lemon rind, salt and nuts, adding enough egg to bind. Stuff the mixture into the hearts and tie them up with strong thread to keep the stuffing in place. Brown the hearts in two tablespoonfuls of oil. Arrange in a baking dish surrounded by the onions. Pour the oil from the pan over the onions and add the stock. Cover and cook in a fairly hot oven (400°F.) for about sixty to seventy-five minutes, or until tender. Scatter with chopped parsley before serving hot. Serve any leftovers sliced as cold meat.

(168) **Savory Hearts**

2 calves' hearts or
4 sheep's hearts
2 tbs. oil
1 cup stock, water or vegetable water
½ bay leaf
½ cup sliced onions
2 sliced carrots
½ cup chopped celery
a little grated raw potato
sea salt
chopped parsley

Remove the fat and sinewy parts from hearts. Cut them into eight half-inch slices across the grain. Heat the oil in a pan and brown the sliced hearts. Add the water and bay leaf, cover and simmer gently for one to two hours, or until tender. Prepare and add the onions, carrots and celery. Replace the cover and simmer for about ten minutes. Thicken with some finely grated raw potato, stir well and simmer for a further five minutes. Sprinkle lightly with salt and chopped parsley.

(169) **Herb Meat Cakes**

1 lb. good quality ground meat
2 tbs. chopped chives
½ tsp. dried or 1 tsp. fresh thyme
1 beaten egg
2 tbs. soya flour

Mix all the ingredients well together in a bowl and form the mixture into thin flat cakes. Coat them with soya flour and broil, bake or sauté them in oil until nicely brown on both sides. Serve hot or cold.

(170) **Kidneys in Apple Juice**

3 calves' kidneys
soya milk (73)
½ cup chopped green onion tops
3 tbs. oil
½ cup apple juice
sprinkle of sea salt

Remove the fat from the kidneys, trim off the hard portion, slice them thinly and leave to soak in a little soya milk for one hour. Sauté the onion in the oil for three minutes. Remove the kidney slices from the milk and dry them on towelling. Add the slices to the pan and cook quickly for two or three minutes, browning on each side. Add the apple juice to the pan and boil it up fast, blending the juices and the onion. Pour the sauce over the kidneys. Add a sprinkle of salt and serve on a heated dish surrounded by emerald potatoes (285).

(171) Kidney and Beans

2 tbs. dried beans
1 bay leaf
2 cloves
2 tbs. oil
1 chopped onion
¾ lb. beef kidney
4 tomatoes
1 tsp. molasses
pinch of sea salt

Cover the beans with water and place in the refrigerator to soak overnight. Next day add the bay leaf and cloves and cook the beans for two to three hours until nearly tender. Heat the oil and cook the chopped onion in it until tender and golden. Skin the kidney and cut it into small cubes, then add to the pan and brown lightly all over. Add the beans, tomatoes, molasses and salt, bring to a boil and simmer gently until the beans are quite tender.

(172) Kidney and Beef Leftovers

1½ cups leftover brown gravy
1 unpeeled scrubbed and grated potato
1 grated carrot
1 finely-sliced onion
pinch of mixed herbs or marjoram, thyme and parsley
½ bay leaf
1 tsp. sea salt
1 cup leftover roast beef or heart
1 cup lamb or beef kidney

Heat the gravy, add the prepared vegetables and seasonings and cook until tender. Dice the beef and then add it to the pot. Remove the hard membranes from the kidneys and cut the kidneys into small cubes. Stir the cubes into the stew and cook for three to five minutes longer. Serve ringed by emerald potatoes. (285).

(173) **Kidney and Mushrooms**

4 lambs' kidneys, halved
2 tbs. oil
1 onion cut in rings
½ cup sliced mushrooms
½ tsp. lemon juice
1 tsp. soya flour
4 tbs. stock or water
½ tsp. sea salt

Cut the membranes from the kidneys and discard them. Sauté the kidneys in hot oil for two minutes. Add the onions and mushrooms and sauté for another minute, then add the rest of the ingredients and mix well. Cover and simmer gently for eight to ten minutes. Sprinkle with salt and serve scattered over emerald potatoes (285).

(174) **Liver and Beef Loaf**

½ lb. liver, cut in slices
½ lb. beef, cut in slices
4 tbs. soya flour
2 tbs. oil
1 onion
Preheat oven to 350°F.
1 stalk celery with leaves
¼ cup grated raw potato
1 egg
1 pureed raw tomato
1 tsp. sea salt
pinch of mixed herbs

Dredge the liver and beef in the soya flour. Heat the oil, sauté the slices quickly and set them aside. Mince the onion and celery. Turn them into the pan used to sauté the meat, cover and stew for eight minutes. Meanwhile mince the liver and beef and add to the vegetables with the grated raw potato, the rest of the soya flour, lightly beaten egg, pureed tomato and seasonings. Mix thoroughly, put into a loaf pan well brushed with oil and bake in a moderate oven (350°F.) for about forty minutes. Serve hot or cold.

(175) **Liver Sticks**

1 lb. pig's liver
1 lb. fresh pork belly
oil to brush utensils
1 large finely chopped onion
pinch of dried sage or a couple of fresh leaves
2 whole eggs
½ tsp. grated nutmeg
mashed potato as required

Mince the liver and pork coarsely and put them into a heavy pan brushed with oil, with the chopped onion and sage. Season with salt to taste. Cook over a low heat (250°F.) for about thirty minutes, to brown all over, stirring occasionally to prevent burning. Pour off the juices and mix the meat with the beaten eggs, nutmeg and enough mashed potato to make a stiff but easy-to-handle mixture. Re-season if necessary after tasting. Shape into small faggots. Lay them side by side in an oiled, oblong casserole, pour the stock over them and cook in a moderate oven (350°F.) until nicely brown, about fifty minutes.

(176) **Liver and Prunes**

1 lb. calves' liver, trimmed and sliced thinly
1 to 2 tbs. soya flour to coat
2 tbs. oil
1 tbs. chopped onion
4 tbs. prunes, soaked overnight, drained and chopped

Dredge the liver in soya flour. Heat the oil in a heavy pan and brown the liver slices on both sides for about five minutes. Add the onions and simmer till transparent. Add the prunes and heat thoroughly. Serve with emerald potatoes (285).

(177) **Liver Slices**

1 lb. beef liver
2 tbs. oil
paprika or soya flour for dredging

Trim the liver and remove any membranes. Cut into half-inch slices. Dredge with paprika or soya flour and sauté for not more than three minutes on each side.

(178) **Malay Curried Chicken Livers** (no curry powder)

3 tbs. oil
1 shallot or small onion, chopped
¾ lb. chicken livers
1 tsp. ground ginger
1 tsp. allspice
2 tbs. raisins
1 tsp. sea salt

Heat the oil in a pan and fry the onion for about ten minutes or until brown. Add the livers and cook for three minutes longer. Mix the ginger, allspice, raisins and salt, put them into the pan and simmer for two minutes more. Serve with a green salad and steamed potatoes.

(179) **Ground Beef with Cabbage**

3½ tbs. oil
1 lb. lean ground beef
1 large onion
1 chopped carrot
1 chopped parsnip
¼ pint vegetable water
sea salt to taste
1 raw potato
1 cabbage
1 tsp. crushed caraway seeds (optional)

Heat 2 tbs. of the oil and fry the beef for three minutes, stirring constantly. Set aside. In the same pan lightly fry the onion, carrot and parsnip. Add the water and salt and grate in the raw potato. Simmer until just tender, sprinkle on to the beef and heat up. Meanwhile wash, dry and shred the cabbage. Steam it on a rack over the minimum amount of boiling water for five to seven minutes. Turn out, mix in the remaining oil and seeds (if used). Make a ring of cabbage on a serving dish and fill the center with the meat.

(180) **Chopped Beef with Carrots and Onions**

2 tbs. oil
2 grated carrots
2 grated onions (or cucumber)
1 lb. lean chopped beef
sea salt to taste
2 tbs. chopped parsley
½ to 1 cup stock or water

Heat the oil in a pan and sauté the grated carrot and onion lightly till crisp. Set aside. Break up the beef with a fork, sprinkle with paprika and sauté in the same pan, turning frequently, for about four minutes till all pinkness has gone. Add the sautéed carrot and onion, parsley and sea salt to taste, and sufficient water to make moist but not sloppy. The meat should be in small biteable lumps, not like a paste.

(181) **Ground Meat Roll** (steamed)

2 cups ground meat
1 small cup grated raw sweet potato
1 tsp. mixed herbs
1 grated carrot
sea salt to taste
1 beaten egg

Mix all the ingredients well and bind with beaten egg. Pack into a large, rimless, oiled jam jar or pudding bowl and cap with parchment paper secured by a rubber ring. Steam for two to two-and-a-half hours. Chill, slip the meat out on to a dish and cut it in slices. Serve hot garnished with watercress or parsley, or use cold for picnic sandwiches.

(182) **Beef-stuffed Apples**

4 large cooking apples
1 grated onion
sea salt to taste
1 lb. minced meat
2 tbs. oil

Preheat oven to 350°F.
Wipe the apples clean, cut off the tops and scoop out the flesh leaving a firm shell. Remove the cores and chop the flesh, mix with the grated onion and beef and add salt. Sauté lightly in oil, then use the mixture to stuff the apple shells. Replace the apple tops as "lids." Set in a dish containing a little water and bake at 350°F. for one hour.

(183) **Beef-stuffed Cucumber (or Squash)**

1 large cucumber or small squash
2 cups cooked ground beef (seasoned)
2 tbs. oil
1 chopped onion
1 tbs. potato or lentil flour
1 cup stock or vegetable water
½ tsp. sea salt
1 tbs. soaked seedless raisins

Peel and cut a piece out of the side of the cucumber, scoop out all seeds with a spoon and stuff the cavity with the meat. Fit back the cut-out piece and tie with strong thread. Heat the oil and sauté the onion and flour until brown. Add the stock, salt and raisins. Place the cucumber in this and simmer till tender. Cut into thick slices and serve with parsley sauce (237) poured over.

(184) **Mock Sausage** (1)

¾ lb. raw lean beef
1 egg
½ cup cooked sweet potato
1/3 tsp. crushed herbs
sea salt as required

The night before, mince the beef, then stir in the potato, herbs and salt. Pound to a paste with the beaten egg and pack into a straight sided jar about two-and-a-half inches across. Leave in the refrigerator till next morning. Slice and fry like commercial sausage meat. Serve for breakfast with fried mushrooms and potato cakes (205) or apple slices.

(185) **Mock Sausage** (2)

1 whole egg
1 grated raw onion
1 tsp. salt or 2 slices
  finely chopped bacon
1 lb. raw ground beef
mashed potato to thicken
a little soya flour
2 tbs. oil

Beat the egg well in a medium bowl and grate in the onion. Add salt and stir in the beef. Add enough mashed potato to form a firm dough. Spread on a potato floured board and roll out to one inch thick. Cut into strips then roll in the palms into finger-long sausages. Roll the sausages in soya flour and brown in hot oil on all sides without covering the pan. Serve hot for breakfast or other meals, or cold, to be eaten in the fingers for picnics.

(186) **Mushroom Beefburgers**

1 egg
1 lb. ground beef
4 oz. finely minced mushrooms
1 tbs. soya flour
1 tbs. minced onion
1 tsp. oil

Beat the egg and use it to bind all the other ingredients together. Divide the mixture into eight flat cakes. Brush them lightly with oil and broil until golden brown on both sides. Garnish with watercress and serve with sautéed tomatoes.

(187) **Stuffed Onions**

1 tbs. oil
2 tbs. mashed potato
¼ lb. minced lean raw meat
¼ lb. minced lean raw bacon (nitrite-free)
1 small sweet pepper, seeded and chopped finely
¼ tsp. paprika
½ pint stock or salted water
4 large onions

Preheat oven to 400° F.

Heat the oil, add all ingredients except the onions and cook until all liquid is absorbed. Remove the outer skin of the onions and scoop out the centers with a teaspoon (reserve for some other dish). Stuff the onions with the meat mixture, set them in a casserole, cover and cook at 400°F. for one hour. Reduce the heat to 350°F. for a further half hour.

(188) **Beef Tongue with Caper Sauce**

1 beef tongue
2 tbs. lemon juice
1 tbs. seedless raisins
1 cup fresh mushrooms, chopped
1 stick celery, chopped
1 chopped parsnip
1 chopped onion
2 chopped carrots
2 tbs. capers (or nasturtium seeds)
a little potato flour

Soak the tongue overnight. Next day wash it and put it into a pan with sufficient water to cover. Add the lemon juice and raisins and bring slowly to a boil. Cover tightly and simmer for two-and-a-half hours, adding a little more lemon juice if needed. Add the chopped vegetables and cook for half an hour longer. The tongue is ready when it is tender to touch and skins without difficulty. Drain it thoroughly, reserving the stock and vegetables. Remove the skin and gristle and cut the tongue into medium thick slices. To make a sauce strain off the vegetables and put them through a sieve. Return them to the stock and add the capers with a little potato flour to thicken if desired. Re-heat and serve the slices covered with the sauce with mashed potatoes, pureed Jerusalem artichokes and watercress. Reserve some slices for cold tongue before adding the sauce.

(190) **Potato Puffs** (Meat Leftovers)

2 cups mashed potato
2 eggs
2 tbs. soya flour
sea salt to taste
2 cups finely chopped meat leftovers
potato flour to dust board
2 tbs. oil

Mix the potatoes, egg, soya flour and salt to make a firm paste and roll it out on a board dusted with potato flour. Cut into rounds with a saucepan lid. Put some meat on one half and fold the other half over like a puff. Pinch or nick neatly all round. Heat the oil in a pan and fry the puffs until light brown. Turn and brown the other side. Serve with home-made tomato sauce (240) and chopped parsley.

(192) **Beef Stroganoff**

1 lb. lean ground beef
2 tbs. oil
½ lb. chopped mushrooms
dash molasses
sea salt to taste
1 tbs. lemon juice in ¼ cup soya milk (73)
chopped parsley

Break up the beef with a fork and toss in hot oil in a pan for about three minutes until browned. Add the mushrooms and simmer for ten minutes. Sprinkle with salt and a dash of molasses. Stir in the lemon juice and soya milk and re-heat, but do not boil. Sprinkle with plenty of chopped parsley. Serve surrounded by emerald potatoes (285) with a green salad.

(193) **Pickled Pig's Feet** (cold)

8 pigs' feet
3 cups water
1 cup lemon juice
¼ to ½ tsp. pickling spice (with no MSG)
1 to 2 tsp. sea salt

Ask the butcher to chop the pigs' feet well. Simmer them in water, seasoning and lemon juice for about three hours without letting the meat fall off the bones. Remove the pigs' feet and put them in a glass dish. Pour the broth into a bowl and cool. When the fat has risen to the surface skim it off and discard it. Liquefy the jellied broth by heating, pour it over the pigs' feet and as soon as they are cool put them into the refrigerator and leave lightly covered for three days. Serve chilled with a potato and green leaf salad. Pickled pigs' feet are an excellent cheap source of calcium.

N.B.—Do not prevent access of air by *close* covering as this could cause dangerous bacteria to thrive.

Chapter 11

MISCELLANEOUS

(194) **Agar-Agar Powder**

This sea weed is used to make a jelly that sets in half an hour. It can be re-heated. The jelly is not so clear as one made with gelatin but if used with fruit this is immaterial. To prepare the jelly take one rounded teaspoonful of the powder and one cup of boiling liquid (water, fruit juice, etc., as required), soften the powder in a tablespoonful of cold liquid, then boil for one minute in hot liquid.

N.B.—Agar is preferable to gelatin which is over-rich in glycine.

(195) **Apple Rings (Home-made)**

apples as available (use fully ripe eating apples)
2 cups cold water
¼ cup lemon juice
1 tsp. vitamin C powder

Dissolve the vitamin C powder in the water in a bowl and add the lemon juice. Wash and wipe the apples. Remove the cores with an apple corer or potato parer. Do not peel (unless the apples have not been organically grown and are sprayed). Cut into quarter-inch slices and leave in the solution for about five minutes, then drain on paper towels or towelling. Thread the slices on clean string hung across your oven and leave to dry at 120°F. to 150°F. with the door propped open and the oven on the lowest setting. This can take about five hours but may need longer. The dry slices should be light colored, dry, yet soft when ready.

Leave them hanging to cool for about twelve hours then pack them into cardboard boxes and store in a dry place, to be used as they are or in cooking.

(196) **Batter (plain)**

5 tbs. split pea flour
pinch sea salt
2 tsp. oil
water as required

Mix flour, salt and oil, adding water to make cream-like mixture. Beat well and set aside for several hours before use to allow absorption.

(197) **Baking Powder (grain-free)**

1 part tartaric acid
1 part bicarbonate of soda
2 parts potato, split pea or lentil flour

Mix together, rub through a dry strainer twice and store in an airtight tin or screw-topped jar.

(198) **Chestnuts (plain)**

Boiled chestnuts have a high iron, vitamin B1 (thiamine) and starch content and are low in fat. Place the unshelled nuts in cold water, bring to the boil and continue for about twenty minutes or until the nuts are tender, and drain well. The nuts are delicious eaten like a boiled egg held in the palm of the hand, with a pinch of salt. They may be carried in a small flat box—include a small spoon.

Carob Flour

Carob flour has nearly three times as high a fiber content as barley or corn and is rich in natural unrefined plant sugar, which is an energy food. Unlike cocoa and chocolate it is free from caffeine. Carob flour is palatable as well as nourishing and is as useful as wheat bran. Use it to replace chocolate, cocoa and Ovaltine in shakes or hot drinks and in cakes or biscuits, but as it has a stronger flavor than chocolate, use rather less. (See also p. 20.)

(199) Coconut Shreds (Home-made)

Open a fresh coconut. Pour off the juice and use it for fruit salads, as a milk substitute or to make shakes (see Beverages). Cut off the brown shell and cut the flesh into one-inch cubes and shred a few at a time in a blender. Or cut the coconut in pieces unshelled and shred it like a carrot on a stainless steel grater. Do *not* add sweetening. Stored in a glass jar with a tight screw lid, the shreds will keep for several days in the refrigerator. For longer storage, dry slowly in the oven with gentle heat.

(200) Instant Apple Chutney

- 2 raw cooking apples, cored and finely chopped
- 2 tbs. chopped sweet peppers, seeded
- 2 tbs. grated onion
- 2 tbs. raisins, pitted and quartered
- 1 tsp. sea salt
- 2 tbs. lemon juice
- 2 tbs. honey
- 1 tsp. ground ginger (optional)
- 1 clove garlic, finely chopped (optional)

Mix thoroughly and serve with cold dishes. Keep refrigerated.

(201) Instant Apple and Banana Chutney

- 2 cooking apples, cored and finely chopped
- 1 banana peeled and thinly sliced
- 1 onion, finely chopped or grated
- ½ tsp. sea salt
- 1 tsp. lemon juice
- 2 tbs. seedless raisins, finely chopped
- pinch of ground ginger

Mix all ingredients thoroughly in a bowl. Turn into a glass dish and serve with cold dishes. Keep refrigerated.

(202) Instant Tomato Chutney

- 3 chopped raw medium tomatoes
- 1 cup freshly shredded coconut
- 1 finely chopped or grated raw onion
- pinch of sea salt
- grating of nutmeg
- 1 grated raw cooking apple
- 1 tbs. finely chopped raisins
- ½ tsp. lemon juice and grated rind of ½ lemon
- dash of honey

Mix thoroughly in a bowl and serve with any cold dishes. Keep refrigerated.

(203) **Mincemeat for Christmas** (no pastry)

½ cup dried beans
½ cup seedless raisins
½ cup diced pears
1 cup diced apples
5 cups water
1 tsp. cinnamon
½ cup ground ginger
½ tsp. sea salt
2 tbs. peanut butter
½ lb. chopped cooked chestnuts

Put all ingredients together in a large heavy pan and simmer for two hours. Serve hot or cold in dessert dishes instead of traditional mince pies at Christmas.

(204) **Potato Batter**

4 tbs. potato flour
pinch of sea salt
2 tsp. oil
2 tbs. warm water
1 egg white

Mix the potato flour and salt with the oil, adding enough water to give a "dropping" consistency. Beat the egg white stiffly and fold in lightly just before using to coat fish, etc., or to make droppies. (For other droppie recipes see chapters 3 and 4.)

(205) **Potato Cakes (Savory)**

1 lb. potatoes
1 tbs. Magic milk (77)
2 tsp. oil
sea salt and dried herbs to taste
paprika or turmeric
2 tbs. oil

Steam the scrubbed, unpeeled potatoes and mash with the Magic milk and oil. Add salt and herbs to taste. Shape into four flat cakes and set out on a dry plate. Sprinkle lightly with paprika (or turmeric) and pat this in. Set aside for at least two hours to allow the surface to dry, then sauté in heated oil and serve under either poached or scrambled eggs, bacon, or baked beans.

(206) **Raw Potato Pancake** (for breakfast)

4 medium potatoes
2 tbs. vegetable oil
sprinkle of sea salt

Scrub the potatoes well. Do not peel them. Grate them

with a stainless steel grater on to a pastry board. Shape in a round to the size of your largest frying pan. Press the cake and pat it hard with a paper towel to draw out the moisture. Place it carefully in the heated oil in the pan and fry until it is cooked inside and both sides of the outside are well browned. Lift out with a spatula and cut into four wedges. Place under bacon, scrambled or poached eggs and so on instead of toast.

(207) **Toast Fingers** (in place of bread toast)

Wash and scrub an old waxy potato. Steam it till nearly tender and drain well. Peel and leave until cold. Cut in bread-thick slices and pat dry on a pastry board with a towel. Toast the slices under the broiler or on a wire rack on the stove. Serve in a toast rack. The slices can be carefully cut into fingers for eating with boiled eggs, etc.

(208) **Potato Pastry (savory)**

1 to 1½ lb. steamed or left-over potatoes
1 scant tbs. oil
1 egg, separated

Preheat oven to 425°F.
Rub the potatoes while warm (re-heat leftovers) through a sieve. Before they are quite cold mix in the oil. Stir in the well-beaten egg yolk. Spread the mixture over any cooked fish, meat or vegetable pie and rough it in curves with a fork. Brush over with the beaten egg white and bake until golden brown in a very hot oven at 425°F.

(209) **Rose-hip Extract**

Gather the rose hips, chill them and remove the blossom ends, stems and leaves. Wash them quickly and measure them into a cup. For each cup of hips boil one-and-a-half cups of water. Add the hips, cover and simmer for fifteen minutes. Mash with a fork or potato masher and allow to stand for twenty-four hours. Strain off the extract through a strainer into a pan and bring to a rolling boil. Add two tablespoons of lemon juice for each pint and boil for five minutes. Pour into warm jars, seal and store in the *dark* to preserve vitamin C.

(210) **Spanish Omelet**

4 unpeeled potatoes
1 bunch spring onions
1 small sweet pepper
pinch of sea salt
6 eggs
2½ eggshells of cold water
2 tbs. oil

Dice the potatoes into half-inch cubes. Skin the onions and cut in half if they are large. Open the sweet pepper, carefully remove the seeds, and shred it. Break the eggs into a bowl, add the water measured in a half eggshell (as a handy measure). Season the eggs and beat with a fork just enough to break and mix the yolks and whites. Heat the oil in a pan and fry the potatoes slowly until nearly tender, add the onions and sweet pepper and fry until all are light brown and tender. Pour the egg mixture on to the vegetables and cook the omelet, stirring it to start with over a fairly brisk heat until it sets solid. Chill. Pack between plates or in a flat container and serve cut in wedges for picnics, etc.

(211) **Stuffing** (vegetable only)

1 cup chopped celery
½ cup mushroom stalks and pieces
½ cup diced young carrots
2 tbs. oil
herbs to taste

Sauté the vegetables lightly in the heated oil. Add any desired herbs (parsley, marjoram, thyme, etc.). Combine all ingredients and use to stuff poultry.

Sugar Substitutes

In any suitable recipe substitute either one cup of minced

raisins or dates or one cupful of honey for half a cupful of sugar. Honey contains a certain amount of moisture so reduce the quantity of any other liquid in the recipe by a suitable amount according to the consistency of the honey. Bake at low temperatures as honey caramelizes fast.

Butter Equivalent

Substitute peanut, olive, safflower, sesame, soy or sunflower (but *never* corn) and reduce the amount slightly:

1 tsp. butter = 1 scant tsp. oil
2 tbs. butter = 1½ tbs. oil
1 cup butter = ⅞ cup oil, etc.

Chapter 12

ONE-DISH MEALS

One-dish meals have a number of advantages. (1) They require only one cooking receptacle which means a saving in fuel and involves less labor in washing up afterwards. (2) They provide under one cover (a) fluids as gravy to quench thirst and replace fluid loss from the body; (b) solids in the form of meat, fish or vegetables to supply protein for repair and maintenance, carbohydrates for energy, and minerals and vitamins for general duties in the body. (3) They can be garnished with raw green vegetables which provide vitamin C.

(212) **Breast of Lamb Stew**

½ cup lentils
2 tbs. dried beans
1 or 2 breasts of lamb
2 large potatoes
1 turnip (not too old)
4 carrots
4 onions
2 crushed bay leaves
handful of parsley (or 1 tsp. mixed dried herbs)
1 tsp. sea salt
2 tbs. finely chopped parsley

Soak the lentils and beans in three pints of water overnight. Trim excess fat from the breasts and cut them into chops. Put into a pot and add the lentils, beans and soaking water and simmer for two-and-a-half hours. Scrub the potatoes, turnips and carrots (only peel them if the skins are rough). Chop all vegetables and drop them into the boiling pot. Add herbs and salt and simmer again until the potatoes are tender. Serve very hot in large soup plates sprinkled with finely chopped parsley.

(213) **Chicken Salad**

1 lettuce, chilled
¼ bunch watercress, chilled
1 small sweet red pepper cut into strips and chilled
4 green olives, chopped
8 spring onions with green tops, chopped
2 chicken breasts cut in thin strips
2 hard boiled eggs, finely chopped
2 cups diced cooked potatoes
1 cup desired salad dressing (see pp. 104-106)

Tear the greens into bite size pieces and throw them into a large serving bowl. Combine with the rest of the ingredients, pour the chosen dressing over and toss well before serving at once.

(214) **Ground Beef and Vegetable Stew**

1 large onion
4 scrubbed, unpeeled potatoes
2 scrubbed, unpeeled carrots
1 to 2 tsp. sea salt
½ bay leaf
2 tbs. oil
1½ to 2 pints stock or water
1 lb. lean ground beef
2 tbs. chopped parsley

Finely chop or grate the vegetables. Heat the oil in a pan and add all ingredients except the beef and parsley. Simmer gently for about ten minutes and set aside. Break up the beef with a fork and cook for about five minutes, stirring all the time. Add the vegetables, with a little water if necessary, and bring to the simmering point again. Sprinkle on the chopped parsley and serve in soup plates.

(215) **Pork and Peas**

1 cup dried split peas
3½ pints water
1 lb. salt pork
2 onions
½ tsp. ground ginger
1 tsp. marjoram
sea salt
sprinkle of chives

Rinse the peas well in cold running water and put them into a large saucepan with the water. Cover and leave in a cold place overnight. Next day bring the peas to the boil, remove from the heat, skim off any pea castings floating on top and then simmer, covered, for two hours. Cut the pork into two-inch squares. Peel and roughly chop the onions. Add the pork, onions, ginger, marjoram and seasoning to the peas, bring to a boil, cover and continue to simmer for a further hour or until the pork is really tender. Serve in wide soup plates sprinkled with chopped chives.

(216) **Potato and Egg Salad**

2 or 3 large waxy potatoes
2 carrots
1 small onion or bunch of chives
4 tbs. oil
2 tsp. lemon juice
pinch of sea salt
dash of honey (optional)
½ clove garlic (optional)
4 hard boiled eggs
1 tomato
chopped parsley

Steam the potatoes over a minimum quantity of water until cooked. Peel and dice them while warm. Grate the carrots and onion (or scissor cut the chives). Blend the oil, lemon juice, salt and honey. Rub a salad bowl with a cut slice of garlic clove (if desired), pour the dressing into the bowl and stir in the potatoes, onion and carrots. Garnish with sliced eggs and sliced tomato and sprinkle with chopped parsley.

(217) **Rabbit Hotpot**

4 cups mixed vegetable soup (253)
1 egg white
½ tsp. sea salt
½ cup mashed potato or potato flour
1 cup minced rabbit (left-overs)
1 cup chopped chives or parsley

Heat the soup. Beat the egg white and add the salt, potato and rabbit. Mix well, form into small balls, drop them into the hot soup and simmer for about ten minutes. Sprinkle on the chives and parsley and serve in deep soup plates.

(218) **Sardine Salad**

4 medium potatoes (steamed)
2 tbs. chopped chives
4 tbs. French dressing (221)
1 cup shredded raw young parsnip or kohlrabi
1 cup shredded raw beets
1 cup shredded lettuce
12 sardines
8 radishes
2 hard boiled eggs

Dice the potatoes, add the chives and toss in the dressing. Shred the parsnip (or kohlrabi), beet and lettuce and toss each separately in dressing. On a large dish set out four rings of potato and put three sardines on each. Surround each ring by little heaps of parsnip, beet and lettuce. Thinly slice the radishes and eggs and use to garnish.

(219) Shrimp and Crab Stew

2 tbs. each grated or chopped parsley, onion, carrot, celery
2 tbs. oil
1 lb. cooked crab or lobster meat (fresh, frozen or canned) coarsely chopped
½ pint cooked shrimp, chopped
1 cup vegetable stock or water
½ tsp. thyme
2 tbs. mashed potato
grating of nutmeg
sea salt to taste
3 tbs. apple juice
sprigs of parsley

Sauté the grated vegetables in one tablespoon of the oil till soft. Add the crab, shrimp, stock and thyme. Simmer for about five minutes but do not boil. Stir the remaining tablespoon of oil into the mashed potato, add a little of the hot liquid and stir well before returning to the pan with the rest of the ingredients. Take out one cup of the mixture and liquidize it lightly then return it to the pan and stir it in. Reheat and serve garnished with parsley sprigs.

(220) Shrimp, Potato and Pea Salad

4 large potatoes, steamed and drained
2 cups freshly podded young peas
½ cup mayonnaise (223, 224, 225)
1 bunch watercress
2 pints cooked shrimp

Dice the potatoes into a bowl and add the raw peas. Pour the mayonnaise over and mix well. Arrange the watercress to circle the edge of a large dish. Add the shrimps to the contents of the bowl, turn into the center of the dish and serve.

Chapter 13

SALADS FOR ALL SEASONS

According to Chambers 20th Century Dictionary a salad is "a preparation of raw herbs, (lettuce, endive, chicory, celery, mustard and cress, watercress, onion, radishes, tomatoes, chervil, etc.) cut up and seasoned with salt, etc." showing that although cold potato and Russian salads are useful ways of using leftovers, they are not strictly entitled to call themselves salads.

We can expand this list of "raw herbs" so as to provide a real salad daily throughout the year without having to pay exorbitant prices for any out-of-season ingredients. To use lettuce as the only green leaf makes for monotony and can be ruinously expensive in winter. Not only are there many other green leaves that offer far better value, but many vegetables and fruits can supplement them, or take their place, to provide the vitamin C for which salads are so valuable. Pigs, deprived of vitamin C because their food has been overcooked or contains none, react by losing the curl to their tails. It is a pity perms don't react in the same way. What a health-and-beauty-building run that would cause on salads, which also give us vitamin A, folic acid, catalase and lysine, four nutrients largely destroyed by cooking, which lessens the vitamin content of any food.

AVAILABLE FOR SALADS

Spring

Leaves. Mustard, cress, summer spinach, lettuce, chives, parsley, mint, lemon balm, garlic mustard (*Alliaria petiolata*),

watercress, chickweed (*Stellaria media*), dandelion (*Taraxacum officinale*).
Flowers or fruit. Broccoli, cauliflower, sweet peppers.
Roots. Spring onion, radish.

Summer

Leaves. Lettuce, cabbage, especially Summer Monarch which, together with red cabbage, is the nicest raw, parsley, mint, lemon balm, watercress, chives, nasturtium.
Flowers or fruit. Cauliflower, broccoli, ridge cucumber, young peas, tomatoes.
Roots. Beet, leek, radish, carrot, onion.

Autumn

Leaves. Cabbage (Autumn Monarch), celery, savoy, endive, lettuce, dandelion, red cabbage.
Flowers or fruit. Tomatoes, broccoli.
Root. Beet, carrot, kohlrabi, parsnip, radish, white turnip, rutabaga, onion.

Winter

Leaves. Cabbage (especially Winter Monarch), red cabbage, endive.
Flowers or fruit. Broccoli, cauliflower, apples.
Roots. Carrot, beet, white turnip, rutabaga, parsnip, leek, onion.

How to use Leaves
Pick leaves freshly, wash them rapidly but thoroughly and dry them by whirling in a salad basket or in a clean dry cloth gathered up by the four corners and swished about till all moisture has gone. Tear soft leaves and shred hard ones with a sharp knife, put them in a deep bowl and with wooden servers or spoons incorporate the chosen dressing until the leaves are coated. Serve.

If the leaves are gathered on a warm day put them in the refrigerator for an hour or so in a closed plastic bag before preparing the salad. Chives, parsley, mint or lemon balm cut into small pieces with kitchen scissors can be sprinkled over the salad or served in a separate small bowl to be added according to the taste of the individual. Perhaps the most useful first spring leaves are the thinnings from a row of summer spinach which braves the weather that daunts the lettuces and keeps them back. Eaten very young, about two inches long, spinach thinnings are sweet and delicious: judging by the flavor, the oxalic acid has not yet risen in them. Children like to dip the individual leaves into personal tiny dishes of their favorite salad dressing.

N.B. Green leaf vegetables are so seldom served cooked that they should be eaten in salads every day.

How to use Flowers or Fruits

Broccoli and cauliflower need careful washing and drying. Flowerets can then be broken into easy-to-handle bits and served with small bowls of home-made mayonnaise for each person to dip into, or else they can be treated as leaves and coated with the desired dressing in a large bowl. Incidentally, the vitamins in cooked cauliflower are more readily available than those in the raw material. As for tomatoes, we agree with Clement Freud that they are not compatible with lettuce and eat those of our own growing with their skins merely washed and dried. Sliced, sprinkled with a pinch of brown sugar and perhaps a touch of basil, they taste delicious eaten on their own with spoons out of a bowl. If ridge cucumbers are well washed they can be sliced with the peel still on and this prevents their being indigestible. Sousing them with vinegar spoils the delicate flavor; we prefer them with lemon and/or oil and sprinkled with mint or parsley, but others may disagree. Green peas in their youth should never be cooked but they make a delicious addition to any salad. Sweet peppers must have their very pungent seeds removed before use and must not be confused with the hot variety, chili peppers, used in pickling and curries.

Roots

We successfully store roots in dry peat and find them invaluable for a winter salad. Beets, turnip, rutabaga and carrot can all be taken up, dried off and brushed clean of soil, then stowed between layers of dry peat in cartons. Stand the chests on large cans if rats are a possibility. Raw shredded carrots are commonplace, but as with cauliflower, their vitamins are not absorbed by the body so easily as those of cooked carrots, though they are pleasant and popular. Raw shredded beets are better because they contain betaine which can double for choline (part of the vitamin B complex) which may be deficient if too little protein is eaten. It is needed to help the body utilize fat. Cooked for ages and drowned in vinegar beets lose half their charm. Scrub and if necessary peel them, then shred them. This can be done on a stainless steel grater. Kohlrabi, onions, leeks—using about three inches of the green part—and spring onions can all be thinly sliced and added to the salad, but you may prefer to serve them in separate bowls since they are not to everyone's taste. I find that covering members of the onion family in oil and refrigerating for, say, half an hour, removes the "repeater" action, and all grated, shredded and cut-up raw vegetables are best if tossed in a little oil at once to prevent oxidation and loss of vitamin C.

Wild Saladings

The advantage of these is that they cost nothing and can be found when vegetables are not yet available from the garden, or when they are still expensive in the stores. Well washed chickweed (*Stellaria media*), chosen from leaves that are large and tender before flowering begins, makes green sandwiches between slices of home-made meat loaf which are enjoyed by children as well as adults. Most French markets sell dandelion leaves for salad but we have to look for our own *Taraxacum officinale* though they are usually not far off. Choose young leaves for they get bitter in their old age.

N.B. Prepare all salads as soon as possible before

serving. If that is not possible, cover them and place them in the refrigerator until needed.

Special Warning

In the tropics, or wherever there is danger of amoebic infection, it is recommended to dip prepared vegetables to be eaten raw in a solution of chloride of lime. Use five grams (1/6 oz.) to two pints of water. After rinsing the vegetables wash them well in water that has been boiled to remove all trace of the chloride of lime.

Growing Green Salads Indoors

Spread a piece or two of thick paper towelling on a flat dish or plastic tray. Damp it well with water, sprinkle thickly with a single layer of seed—mustard, cress, alfalfa, etc., and set on a window sill. Water lightly every day. When the leaves are ready cut them off evenly with a sharp pair of scissors.

"Wheat grass" is simply ordinary wheat, which can be bought in a health food store, grown in the same way and cut before it gets too long and tough. It can be used in salads or as an edible garnish with any dish, hot or cold. (The grass is, of course, gluten free and grain free.)

Sprouting

Beans (broad, butter, French, mung and soya), lentils, peas (chick and green) and seeds (alfalfa, mustard, radish, unhulled sesame, unhulled sunflower) can be sprouted indoors to provide, throughout the year, a small succession of vegetable foods that are excellent sources of proteins, minerals and vitamins. The seeds need damp, darkness, warmth and ventilation. Select two tablespoons of whole clean beans, peas or seeds. They will swell to double this volume after soaking and eight times as much after sprouting. Place the seeds in a clean glass jar with a wide mouth and cover them with tepid water. Secure a piece of nylon mesh over the mouth of the jar by a rubber band or string and leave the seeds to soak overnight. Then drain thoroughly by inverting the jar. Leave the jar on its side in a *dark* cupboard. Rinse the contents well with tepid water two or three times daily (they must not dry out), drain them and leave the jar on its side. The sprouts are ready to eat in three to nine days according to the variety and the temperature. Beans and peas are ready when the sprout is two to three inches long, and lentil and alfalfa when the sprout has reached one to two inches. Use at once, raw if possible, or add to any hot dish just before serving. The sprouts can be kept for a few days if refrigerated.

SALAD DRESSINGS

(221) French Dressing (plain)

3 tbs. lemon juice
9 tbs. oil*

Shake the liquids in a screw-topped jar until well blended. Vary the dressing by the addition of finely chopped chives, carrot, parsley or any other desired herb.

(222) Green Dressing

2 tbs. chives, chopped
1 spring onion, chopped
handful of parsley, chopped
sprig of mint
1 to 2 cups oil

Blend and store in a screw-topped jar in the refrigerator.

(223) Mayonnaise (Cooked Egg)

2 egg yolks (hard boiled)
2 tbs. lemon juice
1 tbs. finely chopped chives or parsley
pinch of sea salt or dribble of honey as desired
6 tbs. oil

Put the egg yolks through a fine sieve. Place them with the lemon juice, chives (or parsley) and sea salt or honey into a blender and blend lightly. Gradually add the oil, blending until of the desired thickness. If no blender is available, add the sieved yolks to the rest of the ingredients in a screw topped jar and shake thoroughly.

*As throughout this book use peanut, olive, safflower, sesame, soy or sunflower, but *never* corn oil.

(224) **Mayonnaise (Egg)**

1 egg yolk
1 tsp. honey
¼ tsp. sea salt
juice of a large lemon
oil

Blend all ingredients but the oil in a blender for a second or so, then gradually pour in oil until the mayonnaise is of the thickness desired—about ½ pint suffices. The mayonnaise can be stored in the refrigerator in a screw-topped jar.

(225) **Mayonnaise (Eggless)**

2 tbs. soya flour
2 tbs. water
½ tsp. sea salt
1 cup oil
juice of ½ lemon
3 tbs. chopped parsley

Make a smooth paste of soya, water and salt in a bowl standing in a pan of hot water and let it heat. Slowly beat in the oil with a rotary beater. Remove from the heat when thick and add the lemon juice and chopped parsley. Beat until smooth and thick.

(226) **Oil and Lemon Dressing**

1 tbs. oil
1 tbs. lemon juice and a grating of rind
pinch of raw sugar or ½ tsp. honey
pinch of sea salt

Blend all ingredients together.

(227) **Oil and Orange Dressing**

Equal parts oil and orange juice
a little grated peel
pinch of sea salt
honey to taste

Blend all ingredients together.

(228) **Peanut and Honey Dressing**

1 tbs. 100 percent peanut butter
1 tsp. honey
1 tsp. oil
1 tbs. lemon juice

Blend well together.

(229) **Shallot Dressing**

4 small shallots or 1 small onion
½ cup oil
pinch of sea salt

Blend.

SUGGESTIONS FOR SALADS

(230) **Avocado and Celery Heart Salad**

1 crisp lettuce
1 avocado
2 celery hearts
1 raw beet, shredded
oil
a few parsley sprigs

Arrange the lettuce on a large dish. Lay on it alternate thin wedges of avocado and celery heart. Garnish with shredded beet tossed in oil, and parsley sprigs. Serve with plain oil and a sprinkle of sea salt.

(231) **Cucumber Cups**

2 large cucumbers
1 cup chopped tomatoes
2 tbs. French Dressing (221)
1 lettuce
4 small radishes

Cut off each end of the cucumbers and scoop out the pulp to make four cups. Chop the remainder of the cucumber and combine with the tomatoes and dressing. Set on a bed of lettuce and garnish each cup with a petalled radish.

(232) **Potato and Beet Salad**

1 crisp lettuce
2 cups diced steamed potatoes
1 cup grated raw young beet
½ cup chopped chives
2 tbs. oil
1 tbs. lemon juice

Line a large bowl with the lettuce leaves. Mix together the diced potato, grated beet and chopped chives. Toss in oil shaken up with lemon juice in a screw topped jar and pile up in the center of the lettuce.

(233) **Stuffed Sweet Peppers**

4 sweet red peppers
2 tbs. scissored chives
¼ cup mayonnaise (223, 224, 225)
grating of onion
2 cups minced chicken
fish or liver leftovers
1 bunch shredded watercress
black olives

Remove the tops, seeds and hard centers of the peppers, cut and turn back the shell in petal fashion. Mix thoroughly the chives and mayonnaise, grate in a little onion juice, then stir in the minced meat or fish and combine well. Stuff the mixture into the peppers and set each one on an individual plate ringed by watercress and garnished with black olives.

(234) **Winter Lettuce and Bean Sprout Salad**

2 cups bean sprouts (preferably mung) (pp. 103-104)
2 tbs. chopped peanuts
2 celery stalks, finely chopped
juice of ½ lemon
1 tsp. honey
pinch of sea salt
2 to 3 tbs. oil
1 lettuce

Arrange the bean sprouts, peanuts and celery in a salad bowl. Use a blender or rotary beater to make a dressing of lemon, honey, salt and oil. Stir the dressing into the other ingredients in the bowl to coat them well. Surround by lettuce leaves, previously well dried and refrigerated in a covered container. Serve at once.

Further Suggestions for Salads

(Ripe olives can be used in all salads but are not cheap)

1. Thinly sliced leek, using both the white and green parts, shredded dessert apple, and sliced tomato, with oil and lemon dressing (226).
2. Finely shredded raw beet and diced celery or diced or grated apple with mayonnaise dressing (223, 224, 225) on a bed of lettuce or watercress.
3. Finely shredded raw red cabbage with diced apple and celery with oil and apple juice dressing.

4. Shredded cabbage heart and shredded onion tossed in oil and orange or lemon juice.
5. Diced steamed potato and radishes with mayonnaise (223, 224, 225) and mustard and cress or chopped chives or chopped mint.
6. Sprigs of broccoli flowers with oil and lemon dressing (226) for dunking.
7. Very young spinach leaves tossed in one tablespoon of oil, then sprinkled with lemon juice.
8. Shredded cabbage heart in mayonnaise (223, 224, 225), garnished with raw cabbage strips and olives.
9. Well dried lettuce leaves torn in pieces and tossed in one tablespoonful of oil, then sprinkled with lemon juice.
10. Shredded red and white cabbage with oil and lemon (226) or green dressing (222) or mayonnaise (223, 224, 225).

Chapter 14

SAUCES

A. SOUR

(235) Golden Sauce

1 egg yolk
pinch of sea salt
½ cup of hot soya milk (73)
pinch of dried herbs (optional) or chopped parsley or chives

Beat the egg yolk well in a bowl and add the salt. Stand the bowl in a pan of hot water. Pour on the hot soya milk gradually and stir gently until the sauce thickens smoothly. Serve hot with vegetables instead of white sauce. Add herbs, parsley or chives before serving if desired.

(236) Lemon Sauce

2 tsp. arrowroot
juice of ½ lemon (strained)
½ cup warm water
grating of nutmeg
pinch of sea salt

Dissolve the sea salt in the warm water in a pan. Add the rest of the ingredients and stir over a low heat until the mixture reaches boiling point and thickens.

(237) Parsley (or Chives) Sauce

2 egg whites beaten to a peak
pinch of sea salt
onion juice to taste
3 tbs. hot soya milk (73)
½ cup finely chopped parsley (or chives)

Sprinkle the salt into the beaten whites and grate in the onion juice. Gradually add the hot soya milk, beating well until the mixture thickens. Use instead of white sauce on any desired vegetable, etc. Any other herbs can be substituted for the parsley, which may be used alone or in combination with others.

(238) **Savory Sauce**

1 tbs. onion juice
1 tsp. crushed celery seeds or grated celery stalk
4 tbs. oil
grating of nutmeg
pinch of sea salt

Liquidize all ingredients in a blender and serve cold.

(239) **Sesame Sauce (home-made)**

½ cup water
1 cup sesame seeds (whole)
2 tbs. oil
½ cup lemon juice
sea salt to taste

Blend the water, oil and seeds in a blender until smooth. Add lemon juice to taste, adding more water if required and salt as desired.

(240) **Tomato Sauce**

4 ripe tomatoes (fresh or canned)
1 shallot or small onion
pinch of sea salt
dash of honey

Slice the tomatoes and onion and cook them until soft in just enough water to prevent burning. Cool. Stir in salt and honey to taste. Sieve and serve hot or cold.

B. SWEET

(241) **Molasses Sauce**

½ cup blackstrap molasses
2 tbs. soya flour
juice of 2 lemons
1½ tbs. oil

Heat the molasses and beat in the rest of the ingredients. Serve hot with potato pancakes (206) etc.

(242) Date Sauce

8 dates, pitted and chopped
1 tbs. oil
1 cup water

Blend all ingredients in a blender, heat and serve in a pitcher or gravy boat with potato pancakes. (206).

(243) Hard Sauce (no alcohol)

½ cup soya flour
¼ cup set honey
3½ tbs. oil
3 tbs. lemon juice

Mix the soya flour and honey well together in a bowl until smooth. Beat in the lightly warmed oil and lemon juice. Chill and serve with potato pancakes (206) or festive pudding (106), but use sparingly.

(244) Lemon Sauce (sweet or sour)

½ cup water
2 tbs. lemon juice
½ cup soya, pea, potato or lentil flour or more as required
2 tbs. honey (for a sweet sauce)
pinch of sea salt (for a sour sauce)

Put the water and lemon juice in a large bowl and gradually add the flour, beating constantly with a rotary beater. When thickened add the honey or salt a little at a time.

(245) Peanut Sauce

½ cup peanut butter (guaranteed gluten-free)
½ cup soya milk (73)

Beat the peanut butter and soya milk together until quite smooth. Serve as a sauce with potato pancakes (206) etc., adding a little honey if desired.

(246) Rhubarb Sauce

1 cup raw young rhubarb stem, (*never* the leaves) cubed
2 tbs. soya flour
2 to 3 tbs. honey

Blend or sieve and mix together until smooth. Serve with potato pancakes (206) etc.

Chapter 15

SOUPS

Canned soups and dry soup mixes are out on a grain-free diet because they are thickened with white flour, the cheapest filler. But that does not mean that you cannot have honest-to-goodness home-made soups in place of these commercially profitable non-foods.

Home-made soups range from chilled soups made from raw vegetables in summer to hot and lightly cooked varieties in winter. These methods of preparation conserve natural values, flavor and color, and take little time. As a starter on a cold night hot soups set the digestive juices flowing with their delicious aroma and appearance. As a stirrup cup for departing guests facing the darkness after a party they have the priceless advantage over the conventional "one for the road" of warming the very cockles without the risk of making anyone too high to be safe as a driver.

Soup Stock (To be used in place of water or milk in recipes)
Following the methods of the thrifty French we can prepare soup stock by extracting vitamins and minerals from bones and scraps of meat. Simmering, at about 180°F. is the usual procedure, but in fact a higher temperature is preferable for bones since they contain no vitamins to be destroyed and the best method is to cook them in a pressure cooker for 30 minutes. Failing that it is best to boil them for a couple of hours, adding some salt to extract the juices and vinegar to extract the calcium.

However, there is no need to use anything but vegetable

leftovers and discards. Collect any coarse outer leaves of cabbage, broccoli, spinach, lettuce or any other green leaves that are usually thrown away when preparing salads or cooked vegetables, also washed pea shells, stalks of cabbage, celery and so on, with the green tops of leeks and onions. Wash them thoroughly and put them into the refrigerator in a plastic bag with any vegetable parings from well washed vegetables. When ready to make soup, chop the vegetables well, cover them with water and boil slowly for only fifteen minutes to extract the flavors and as many minerals and vitamins as possible. Strain off the liquid and allow it to cool. Use what you require for the soup you have selected and store the rest in screw-topped jars in the refrigerator. It has been demonstrated that boiling for only four minutes draws out magnesium, iron, manganese, potassium, sodium and phosphorus into the water used and during the fifteen minutes suggested the greater part of the minerals will have been transferred to the stock. Incidentally, the nutritive value of any soup can be raised by adding a little soya flour which does not alter the taste but thickens the soup slightly.

To add creaminess without adding flour to soups

(a) Stir a well-beaten egg yolk into a pot of soup when it stops boiling. Stir continuously for two minutes, allowing the soup to heat but not to boil which would curdle the egg.

(b) Stir in a small amount of mashed potato.

(247) **Broad Bean Soup**

- 1 cup shelled broad beans past their first youth
- 1 pint slightly salted water or vegetable stock
- 1 large onion, cut up
- bunch of fresh or pinch of dried herbs
- 1 potato, cut up

Drop the beans into the boiling water with the onion, herbs and potato. Cook until the beans are tender. Remove and cool. Liquidize in a blender and strain off the husks or rub them through a sieve. Thin the mixture to the desired thickness by adding boiling water. Re-heat.

(248) Carrot Soup

2 pints stock or water
½ lb. carrots
1 small potato
sea salt to taste
1 onion

Bring the stock or water to a boil in a pan. Scrub the carrots and potato well, peel the onion and shred them all on a grater gradually into the boiling water. Keep at boiling point for a moment. Cover, lower the heat and cook gently until tender. Add salt to taste and serve.

(249) Clear Vegetable Broth

3 cups water
3 cups finely shredded vegetables
vegetable salt

Use any desired vegetable or combination such as carrot, celery, onion, turnip. Simmer gently until the flavor is extracted and pour through a fine sieve. Season with salt or any preferred herb and re-heat before serving.

(250) Lentil Soup (green)

3 cups stock or water
1 cup whole green lentils
bouquet garni (parsley, thyme, bay leaf)
1 handful parsley
1 tsp. sea salt
1 cup soya milk (73)
1 chopped onion
1 chopped celery stalk

Soak the lentils in water or stock overnight after washing them well. Bring them to a boil with the bouquet garni in the same water or stock and simmer for about three-and-a-half hours or until soft. Drop in the chopped vegetables, add the salt, and simmer for another fifteen minutes. Add the soya milk and sieve or liquidize in a blender. Re-heat and serve with potato croutons (257).

(251) Lentil Soup (yellow)

1 cup split red lentils
3 cups stock or water
1 tbs. oil
1 chopped onion
1 chopped carrot
1 chopped celery stalk
bouquet garni (parsley thyme, bay leaf)
1 tsp. sea salt
1 cup soya milk (73)

Wash the lentils and soak for twenty-four hours in water or stock. Simmer gently for about two hours with the bouquet garni. Heat the oil in a pan and gently sauté the chopped vegetables until crisp, not tender. Add to the simmering lentils with the sea salt and continue cooking for about five minutes longer. Add the soya milk and re-heat. Serve the soup as it is, or after blending with potato croutons (257).

(252) **Minestrone (no rice or pasta)**

3 cups water
½ cup butter beans (soaked overnight)
1 tbs. chopped onion
2 tbs. oil
1 large potato, diced
1 small zucchini, diced
1 garlic clove, crushed (optional)
1 cup cabbage, cut in strips
½ cup diced green beans
pinch of fresh or dried basil
3 tbs. chopped parsley
sea salt to taste

Measure three cups of the water in which the beans have been soaked. Put it into a pan and cook the beans for two to three hours until tender. Sauté the onion in oil until transparent, add the potato and zucchini and sauté for five minutes longer. Add to the pan with the beans, garlic (if used), cabbage and runner beans. Cook until the potato is tender. Add the basil, parsley and salt and cook for three minutes longer before serving.

(253) **Mixed Vegetable Soup**

Have boiling salted water ready in a pan. Throw in a cut-up onion, carrots gently brushed and cut lengthwise, torn-up outer leaves of cabbage, sprouts or broccoli, cut-up potato and any bits of vegetable in season. Five minutes before it is cooked throw in a large handful of cut-up parsley. The soup can be mashed when ready. Serve thick.

(254) **Mushroom Soup**

1 cup finely chopped mushrooms
1 small onion, finely chopped
1 tbs. oil
1 small potato, diced
3 cups water

Lightly sauté the mushrooms and onion in the oil, add the

water and diced potato and simmer for about ten minutes. The soup can be served as it is or liquidized in a blender and re-heated before serving.

(255) **Parsnip Soup**

1 medium parsnip or 2 small ones
2 tbs. oil
2 tbs. chopped onion
1½ cups stock or water
washed onion skin to color pale yellow
1 small cooked potato
chopped chives
sea salt to taste

Peel and dice the parsnip. Heat the oil and add the parsnip and onion. Cover and simmer gently for ten minutes. Do not allow the vegetables to brown. Add the water, onion skin and potato and simmer until the parsnip is tender. Liquidize in a blender and taste for seasoning but keep the flavor mild. Sprinkle with chopped chives and serve.

(256) **Peashell Pottage**

2 lb. fresh young snow peas
1½ pints boiling water
1 small mild onion (or 2 shallots)
pinch of sea salt
dash of honey
1 good sprig of mint

Wash the shells and drop them into boiling water. Peel and chop the onion and add to the pot. Boil until the vegetables are softish. Add the salt and honey and let the soup cool then add a sprig of mint. Liquidize the soup in a blender and press it through a sieve to remove fibers. Re-heat and serve with potato croutons (257).

(257) **Potato Croutons**

1 tbs. lentil or pea flour
1 tbs. cold mashed potato
1½ tsp. oil
2 egg yolks
pinch of sea salt

Mix all the ingredients together in a pan over a very low heat and stir until the mixture thickens. Pour it into a flat dish and when cold stamp it into small shapes and put them in a moderately hot oven (375°F.) to harden and color light brown. Store the croutons in a screw topped jar in the refrigerator. Serve with soups as desired.

(258) **Pumpkin Soup**

1½ lb. pumpkin
1 potato
1 to 1½ pints water
pinch of sea salt
pinch of mixed herbs (optional)

Remove the seeds and rind from the pumpkin and cut it into cubes. Scrub the potato but only peel it if the skin is dark. Boil the potato and pumpkin together in seasoned water until cooked. Remove, cool and liquidize in a blender. Re-heat and serve.

(259) **Quick Clear Soup**

1 onion
1 clove
2 sticks celery
1 carrot
Bouquet garni (1 sprig each thyme, marjoram and parsley) or ½ tsp mixed herbs in bag
2 pints water
pinch sea salt
4 tsp. agar-agar

Chop the onion coarsely and stick the clove into one of the pieces. Chop the celery and carrot finely and add the bouquet garni, salt and water. Bring to the boil and simmer for fifteen minutes. Stir in the agar-agar and simmer for another five minutes. Strain through a fine strainer. If peas are available add them as a garnish.

(260) **Quick Onion Soup**

2 large onions
1 tbs. oil
1 to 2 leftover potatoes, diced
1 tsp. sea salt
1½ pints vegetable stock
washed onion skin to color

Peel and chop the onions finely and sauté them in heated oil until transparent only. Add them with the diced potatoes to the salted stock and drop in a piece of well washed onion skin to give a golden color. Simmer gently, then remove the onion skin and serve very hot.

(261) **Quick Soya Soup**

1 tbs. oil
1 finely chopped onion
1 finely chopped tomato
2 tbs. soya flour
1½ to 2 pints stock or water
sea salt to taste

Heat the oil and sauté the onion and tomato lightly. Make a paste with the soya flour and a little of the liquid. Stir in the rest of the liquid and pour the mixture over the sautéed onion and tomato. Simmer for seven to ten minutes stirring constantly. Add salt to taste before serving.

(262) **Quickest Thick Vegetable Soup**

2 cups water or vegetable stock
2 medium potatoes
2 medium onions
2 large carrots
1 stick celery
pinch of sea salt

Bring the water to a boil in a pan. Grate all the vegetables and drop them into the boiling liquid. Add the sea salt and simmer until the vegetables are tender and crisp—about seven to ten minutes only.

(263) **Quick Vegetable Soup**

2 tbs. oil
2 medium carrots
1 small turnip
1 small parsnip
2 medium onions
1½ pints stock or water
1 sprig each marjoram, thyme, parsley, ½ bay leaf
1 tbs. chopped parsley for garnish
sea salt to taste

Heat the oil in a pan and grate in finely the carrots, turnip, parsnip and onions. Sauté them lightly. Add the stock and the herbs tied in muslin. Simmer gently for a few minutes until tender. Remove the herbs, add salt to taste and reheat. Add finely chopped parsley just before serving.

(264) **Runner Bean Soup**

2 pints water
1 cup elderly runner beans, coarsely chopped
1 large raw potato
sea salt to taste

Bring the water to a boil and drop in the runner beans. Grate in the raw potato, add salt and boil until the beans are tender. Remove from the heat and cool a little. Liquidize in a blender and strain off the fibers or rub the soup through a coarse sieve. Reheat and serve.

(265) **Scotch Broth** (no barley)

½ to 1 lb. neck of lamb
3 pints cold water
1 diced onion
1 diced carrot
1 diced turnip
½ celery stalk
1 diced potato
1 tsp. sea salt
1 tsp. finely chopped parsley

Put the meat into the cold water in a pan and simmer gently for about two-and-a-half hours. Cool. Strip the meat off the bones, cut it into small pieces and replace them in the pan after carefully removing any bone fragments. Add the diced vegetables and simmer until just tender, not mushy. Add the salt and sprinkle with chopped parsley.

(266) **Spinach Soup**

1 lb. spinach
2 pints water or stock
1 large potato
1 small onion
1 cup soya milk (73)
good pinch of sea salt
grating of nutmeg

Wash the spinach thoroughly in several changes of water to remove any grit. Put it into a large pan with the water or stock. Add the well-scrubbed and diced potato and the finely chopped onion. Simmer until the potato is tender. Remove from the heat and cool. Liquidize the soup in a blender or rub it through a sieve. Return it to the pan, add the soya milk, salt and nutmeg, reheat and serve.

(267) **Split Pea Soup**

1½ pints water
1 cup dried split peas
2 potatoes, scrubbed and cut up
dash of honey
1 small carrot, cut up
1 small onion, chopped
sea salt to taste
handful of finely chopped mint leaves

Wash the peas well and discard any dark ones that float. Put the washed peas into a bowl with the water and leave for twenty-four hours, refrigerated if possible. Using the same water, simmer the peas for about one-and-three-quarter hours, adding more water as it boils away. Now add the potatoes, honey, carrot and onion and simmer until all are nearly tender. Add the mint leaves and simmer for five minutes more. Liquidize in a blender and serve with potato croutons (257).

(268) **Summer Soup** (uncooked, served cold)

1 lb. fresh or canned tomatoes chopped in 1 cup of water
½ sweet pepper with seeds removed (preferably red and ripe, not green and unripe)
¼ cucumber
¼ onion or 2 shallots, chopped
1 clove garlic (optional)
1 tsp. honey
sea salt to taste

Wash the vegetables thoroughly, peeling only the onion and garlic, then drop all the ingredients into a blender to blend (or use a Mouli machine). Add more water if too thick. Taste and season if required. Chill the soup in the refrigerator and serve in bowls. (It may also be heated in a pan with the lid on and served hot.)

(269) **Tomato Soup** (chilled)

4 large tomatoes
pinch of sea salt
drip of honey
2 tsp. agar-agar

Liquidize the tomatoes, salt and honey in a blender, or press the tomatoes through a sieve and mix with the other two ingredients. (Reserve the pulp and seeds for gravy or stews.) Soften the agar-agar in a quarter cup of this liquid and dissolve over boiling water. Add to the rest of the liquid, pour into small bowls and chill. Garnish with sprigs of mint or basil.

(270) **Tomato Soup** (hot)

2 cups fresh or canned tomatoes
2 tbs. chopped onion
1 clove
¼ crushed bay leaf
1 small stick celery
2½ cups water
1 cooked potato

Blend all ingredients in a blender and simmer for five minutes. If preferred sieve the soup after liquidizing. Serve hot.

(271) **Vegetable Punch Soup**

2 tbs. oil
1 cup grated onion
1 cup grated potato
1 cup grated carrot
1 cup grated or minced parsnip
3 cups boiling water
1 tsp. sea salt (optional)

Heat the oil in a pan and toss the onion in it until transparent only. Stir in the rest of the vegetables and the boiling water. Cook gently on a low heat until well blended but not soggy. Sprinkle in the salt and serve.

(272) **Vichyssoise** (cold)

1 chopped medium onion
2 tbs. oil
1 diced large potato
3 cups chicken or vegetable stock
nutmeg
sprinkle of sea salt
chopped chives

Sauté the chopped onion in oil until transparent only. Cover the pan and set aside. Simmer the potato in the stock until cooked. Add the onion, salt and a grating of nutmeg, then purée all together in the blender. Chill and scatter with chopped chives before serving.

Chapter 16

SPREADS

(273) **Apricot Spread**

2 tbs. dried apricots
water to cover
1 small apple or pear

Pour sufficient boiling water over the apricots just to cover and leave overnight. Rub the appricots through a sieve (or puree in a blender) and blend in the apple or pear to make a thick cream consistency. Use instead of jam. (A little honey may be added to the mixture.)

(274) **Chicken Liver Spread**

1 cooking apple
1 cup cooked chicken livers
¾ tsp. sea salt
1 large onion, chopped
1 peeled garlic clove (optional)
pinch of powdered rosemary

Core and chop the cooking apple and mix all the ingredients well. Purée in a blender and turn into a glass dish. Cover and refrigerate. Eat within three days.

(275) **Date and Apricot Spread**

1 cup orange juice and pulp
½ cup dried apricots
¼ cup dates, chopped

Pour the juice over the apricots and leave to soak overnight. Next day place them in the blender with the dates and blend until the fruit is finely chopped. Turn the mixture into a jam jar and use as a sweet spread within a week or so.

(276) **Simple Liver Spread**

½ lb. liver
2 tbs. oil
1 chopped onion
1 small grated carrot
4 tbs. water or stock
1 tbs. soya flour
1 sprig parsley

Chop the liver and sauté it in the oil. Sauté the onion and the carrot. Leave to cool. Pour the water into the blender, add the rest of the ingredients and blend to a smooth paste adding more water if required. Turn into a screw topped jar and refrigerate. Use within a reasonable time.

(277) **Mock Chocolate Spread**

1 really ripe banana
2 to 3 tbs. carob flour
pinch of scraped vanilla bean

Mash the banana thoroughly with the carob flour, add the vanilla and beat until quite smooth. Pack the mixture into a small screw topped jar and use in place of jam. The spread keeps for a few days if refrigerated.

(278) **Nut Spread**

1 cup cold water
1 cup chopped nuts (any variety or mixed)
2 tbs. oil
4 tbs. lemon juice
½ tsp. sea salt
squeeze of onion juice
pinch of dried sage (optional)
turmeric or paprika to color

Pour the water into the blender and turn on. Add the nuts gradually and blend until very fine. Gradually add the oil then the lemon juice and blend to the desired thickness. Add the seasonings and enough turmeric or paprika to color the spread attractively. Turn it into a screw topped jar and chill. Use within a few days.

(279) **Onion "Butter"**

1 lb. white onions
1 tbs. oil
1 tbs. arrowroot
½ cup water
½ tsp. sea salt

Peel and cut up the onions finely. Heat the oil, add the

onions to the pan and sauté them gently until transparent but not colored. Remove the onions from the pan, mash them with a fork and return them to the pan. Mix the arrowroot thoroughly with the water, add the salt and add to the pan. Bring the mixture to a boil and simmer for five minutes. Turn into a small glass dish and refrigerate. The "butter" will keep for several days in the refrigerator.

(280) **Potted Meat Spread**

½ cup minced or finely diced left-over heart or kidney
1 small onion, roughly chopped
½ tsp. sea salt
1 lb. soya flour
oil or home-made mayonnaise (223, 224, 225)

Combine all the ingredients gradually, using oil or home-made mayonnaise to moisten. Press into a small glass dish and chill. Use within a few days.

(281) **Sardine Spread**

½ cup sardines with some of their oil
1 tbs. soya flour
1 small onion or shallot or chives, very finely chopped

Pound all ingredients together in a bowl or mortar and press into a small dish. Cover and chill. Use within a few days.

(282) **Shrimp Spread**

20 fresh shrimp
sprinkle of paprika
grating of nutmeg
1 tbs. oil

Peel and chop the shrimps, then grind them thoroughly in a bowl or mortar. Beat the paprika and nutmeg into the oil. Add the pounded shrimps and mix well. Press the mixture into a small glass dish, cover and chill. Use within a few days.

Chapter 17

VEGETABLES

VEGETABLE COOKING (for best nutritional value)

The rules for preparing vegetables are simple and few but important. It is so easy to be a killer in the kitchen, murdering the enzymes, vitamins and minerals committed to our care and necessary for the health of the household. Here is a list of the essential rules and the reasons for them.

Rule	Reason
1. Leave on roots, tops and outer leaves in gathering or buying. Cut off just before washing.	Delays wilting, and vitamin values are increased until the onset of wilting, when they decline.
2. Wash rapidly and thoroughly under the cold tap.	Soaking or using warm water causes loss of vitamins B and C.
3. Drain quickly then pat fruits and roots dry with towelling. Dry leafy vegetables by whirling them in a bag made of towelling or in an old pillow slip.	This prevents minerals, the water soluble vitamins B and C and flavors from passing into the water.

4. Keep washed vegetables in a plastic bag or other closed receptacle in the refrigerator until required.	Prevents attack by oxygen, causing loss of vitamins A, C and E.
5. Keep all vegetables requiring storage in a cool dark place.	Light and warmth can destroy much riboflavin, folic acid and vitamin C.
6. Whenever possible avoid peeling vegetables. Scrub them well with a nylon nail brush.	Many valuable nutrients lie in and under the skin, and are lost in peeling.
7. Never discard liquids from cooking but save them for use in soups and gravies.	These liquids contain extracted minerals and vitamins.

Cooking Vegetables

Boiling vegetables is an insult to both plant and palate that should never be inflicted on either. Flavor, appearance and food value can all be preserved by methods such as the following which apply to all varieties of vegetables.

1. Absolutely accurate pressure cooking according to the instructions issued with the utensil. Over-cooking readily occurs causing unpleasant odors from the release of simple sulphur compounds and destruction of B complex vitamins and vitamin C. Also flavor is lost through expulsion of aromatic oils and damage to proteins. Overcooked vegetables can also cause flatulence and indigestion.

2. Waterless cooking (so-called). This method actually requires a couple of tablespoonfuls of water heated to boiling point to fill the utensil with steam. The vegetable is then dropped in gradually. When the material is heated through the heat is lowered to prevent escape of steam, and the natural water content of the vegetable is sufficient to complete the cooking.

3. Steaming in a steamer or on a rack in a pan. Vegetables should be left unpeeled and uncut if possible to prevent too many minerals and water soluble vitamins dissolving into the water below, which should in any case be kept and used in gravy or soup.

4. Sautéing in a covered pan. One or two tablespoonfuls of oil are heated, the well dried and chilled vegetables are shredded freshly with a sharp knife and dropped in. They are well tossed to coat them with the oil to seal the surfaces against oxygen and when heated through should be covered and cooked at lower heat for about five to ten minutes.

5. Broiling, after brushing with oil, heating through rapidly, then turning to ensure crispness and to prevent shrivelling.

6. Frying well dried and chilled vegetables which are cut up and dropped into deep hot oil has the advantage that cooking time is short and only the natural juices are used but it is not recommended for frequent use and the oil must not be re-used.

7. Baking either in or out of the jacket. This can be used for onions as well as potatoes, beets and parsnips. This method has the disadvantage of slow initial heating and long cooking with consequent loss of vitamin C. The loss can be overcome to some extent if the surfaces are brushed with oil, or if the vegetables are first steamed, and only finished in a pre-heated oven.

Potatoes

Learn to respect the common potato. Although it is predominantly a carbohydrate food, its protein is ranked higher than those found in the cereal grains. So "a liberal amount of potatoes in the diet is preferable to its equivalent in cereals" (Mattice, M. A., Bridges, M. R. *Food and Beverage*

Analyses, Henry Kimpton, London, 1950). In fact, potato proteins have been revealed as a very good source of the essential amino acids, having, except for histidine, a much higher content than whole wheat (Hughes, B. P., *British Journal of Nutrition*, 1958, *12*, 188-95). Numerous nutritional and "balance" experiments with potatoes as the sole source of protein have consistently proved the high protein content (Schuphan, W., *Nutritional Values in Crop Plants*, Faber & Faber, 1965).

Potatoes also provide nearly the same amount of crude fiber as wholemeal bread (*Refined Carbohydrate Foods and Disease*, Edited by Burkitt, D. P., and Trowell, H. C., Academic Press, 1975).

So anyone on a grain-free, milk-free diet is losing nothing but in fact gaining in nutritional value by using potatoes cooked in a wide variety of ways in place of bread, biscuits, breakfast cereals and so on. As always, do *not* use corn oil in recipes requiring oil.

(283) **Baked New Potatoes**

Scrub and dry well small new potatoes, place them on an oiled baking tin or pan and bake them either in the oven or on top of the stove for about twenty minutes, shaking a couple of times to turn them over. Serve sprinkled with sea salt and paprika.

(284) **Crisped Potatoes**

Preheat oven to 425°F.
Scrub potatoes thoroughly without peeling. Shred them coarsely with a potato peeler or on a grater to make shreds from one quarter to one eighth of an inch thick and spread out on paper towels. Fold over the towels and leave it to absorb the moisture. Shake out the potato shreds, place them in an oiled pan and bake until crisp in a hot oven (425°F.). Sprinkle lightly with sea salt.

(285) **Emerald Potatoes**

Scrub four unpeeled potatoes, chill them and then cut them into one-inch chunks. Remove the peel only if you are pedantic about whiteness. Simmer in half a cupful of water in a closed pan for about ten minutes or until soft. Mash well, stir in two tablespoonfuls of finely chopped parsley and remove to a heated dish.

(286) **Gnocchi Potatoes**

4 jacket baked or left-over steamed potatoes
a little potato flour
1 egg
sea salt to taste

Put the potatoes through a food mill or sieve. Mix all ingredients thoroughly to form a stiff dough. Shape the dough into tiny sausage shapes and drop them into a pan of boiling water and cook for three to five minutes after they have risen to the surface. Drain and serve with soft margarine and chopped parsley.

(287) **Broiled Potato Slices**

Select large, waxy potatoes. Scrub them well but do not peel them. Chill them and cut them into thin slices. Brush both sides of each slice with oil and arrange them on an oiled baking sheet under the broiler. Cook for about five minutes or until nicely brown, then turn with a spatula and cook for another three to five minutes until they are brown on the other side. Sprinkle lightly with salt and serve. The slices can also be spread with any savory spread and eaten in place of buttered toast.

(288) **Jacket Potatoes** (baked in the oven)

Preheat oven to 450°F.
Scrub the required number of potatoes and dry them with towelling. Brush them with oil and place them in a hot oven (450°F.) and cook for about forty-five minutes, or until tender when pierced.

(289) **Jacket Potatoes** (broiled and baked)

Preheat oven to 350°F.
Place potatoes prepared as above on a baking sheet under moderate heat. Leave for about fifteen minutes then turn to heat through. Transfer to a moderate oven (350°F.) and

cook for about another fifteen minutes or until they seem tender when pierced by a fork to let out steam.

(290) **Jacket Potatoes** (in pan)

Select long slim potatoes. Scrub them thoroughly and dry with towelling. Brush them all over with oil and put them in a heated pan with two tablespoonfuls of oil. Replace the lid and keep the heat fairly high for five minutes to heat them through, then lower the heat and simmer gently for twenty to thirty minutes until the potatoes are tender when pierced by a fork to let out steam. Leave the lid off for the last five minutes.

(291) **Oven-fried Potatoes**

Preheat oven to 450°F.
Scrub the required number of potatoes and chill them. Do not peel them but cut them into thin sticks. Pat them dry and toss in a bowl with one or two tablespoonfuls of oil. Put them into a hot oven (450°F.) in a baking dish and leave for about eight minutes, then lower the heat and cook until tender. Sprinkle lightly with sea salt before serving.

(292) **Sauté Potatoes**

2 tbs. oil
4 cold raw or cooked potatoes
sprinkle of sea salt or kelp

Heat the oil in a pan. Cut the potatoes into thin slices and drop them into the oil. Cover the pan, toss well and cook until the slices are lightly brown. This will take about five minutes for pre-cooked potatoes and five to ten minutes longer for raw ones. Sprinkle with sea salt and serve.

(293) **Shredded Potatoes (Quick Cooked)**

Shred over a dish towel, then pat dry, four thoroughly chilled, scrubbed, unpeeled potatoes. Heat four tablespoonfuls of oil in a pan and drop in the potatoes. Keep the heat high, turn frequently and cook the shreds for about five to eight minutes until golden brown. Sprinkle with salt and a dash of paprika. If liked, a little shredded onion may be cooked with the potatoes.

(294) **Steamed Potatoes**

Drop the required number of scrubbed, unpeeled small potatoes, or larger ones cut to the same size, into half a cup of boiling water, or place them on a rack above boiling water. Replace the pan lid and cook for about fifteen to twenty minutes or until tender. Cool slightly and peel the potatoes, using a fork to hold them, then return them to the pan to heat up and sprinkle with a little chopped parsley mixed with a little oil and add salt to taste.

(295) **Steamed Unpeeled Potato Leftovers**

Keep the potato leftovers in the refrigerator overnight. Slice them thinly, heat them up in a quarter of a cup of left-over gravy, sprinkle with chopped chives and serve.

(296) **Stuffed Potatoes**

4 leftover medium jacket potatoes

Preheat oven to 400°F.

Scoop out the pulp from the potatoes, add half a teaspoon of sea salt, mash and mix in either grated raw onion or two tablespoons of finely chopped chives or one cup of finely chopped mushrooms, celery or tomatoes and sauté in oil. Pack the mixture into the shells, sprinkle with dried or fresh mixed herbs or paprika and cook for about ten minutes at 400°F.

Or, mix the pulp with four tablespoons of mayonnaise (223, 224, 225) and two tablespoons of chopped parsley, chives, mint or any other herb you fancy, and stuff the shells.

Chapter 18

VEGETARIAN DISHES

As vegetarians rely largely on delicious and nutritious wholemeal wheat bread at most meals, and wholemeal flour in much of their cooking, while they may also eat much more rye, oats, barley, corn, millet and rice than meat eaters, they are likely to feel more of a loss than most of us in being deprived of all cereals and cereal products.

There seems to be no separate record of how many vegetarians are schizophrenia sufferers. But for people caring for vegetarian patients a special warning is due. Today wheat gluten is widely included as a filler in made-up vegetarian foods in order to increase the protein content. This is presumably in order to find a use for the gluten derived as a by-product when white flour is treated to make it gluten-free for the special use of celiacs.

Any vegetarian on a cereal-free diet would be well advised, therefore, to give up all commercial made-up foods (unless they carry a guarantee that they contain no cereals or milk) and to rely entirely on home-made dishes from known ingredients.

Indeed as meat and fish get more and more expensive nonvegetarians could do worse than sample some of the savory vegetarian recipes which follow.

N.B. To ensure an adequate intake of "complete" protein, recipes marked with an asterisk should be supplemented by a dish containing eggs, nuts, soya flour or soya milk in reasonable quantity.

(298) **Stuffed Avocados (Special)**

2 unpeeled avocados
4 tbs. soya cheese (89) or
  4 chopped hardboiled eggs
1½ to 2 tsp. lemon juice
1 tsp. oil
sea salt to taste
cress, lettuce or watercress
sprinkle of paprika

Halve the avocados and remove the pits. Carefully scoop out the flesh and mix it well in a bowl with the soya cheese or chopped eggs, shake together the lemon juice, oil and salt and add to the mixture. Taste for seasoning. Press down the empty skins on individual plates and fill with the mixture. Sprinkle lightly with paprika. Surround by cress or watercress.

(297) **Apple and Coconut Curry** (no curry powder and no rice)

2 tbs. oil
2 finely chopped onions
2 cups chopped tomatoes
1 tbs. raisins
1 tsp. molasses
1 tsp. ground ginger
1 tsp. allspice
2 cored and chopped apples
1 cup shredded coconut

Heat the oil and fry the onions and tomatoes until tender. Add the raisins, molasses and spices and stir well. Cook for one minute. Add the apples and coconut and cook for five minutes. Heap up on a dish, surround with emerald potatoes (285) and serve.

(299) **Bean Casserole**

1 lb. dried beans
⅓ cup chopped onion
½ tsp. chopped thyme
4 tbs. oil
3 whole cloves
¼ tsp. freshly ground pepper
  (optional)
1 cup stock
2 tsp. sea salt

Place the beans in sufficient water to cover them and leave them in the refrigerator for twenty-four hours. Place the soaked beans in a heavy saucepan together with the soaking water. Add all ingredients except the stock and salt. Cover and simmer for one to one-and-a-half hours, stirring occasionally. Add the stock and salt and cook for a further twenty minutes. Serve hot, garnished with chopped chives or parsley.

(300) **Brown Bean Loaf***

2 cups cooked kidney beans
1 cup shredded onion
1 cup shredded celery
1 to 2 tbs. vegetable water
or water
½ cup mashed potato
½ tbs. oil
sprinkle of paprika

Preheat oven to 350°F.
Mash up the beans in a bowl. Add and mix in well the onions, celery and liquid. Pack the mixture into a pie-dish, smooth it down and spread the mashed potato over the surface. Brush with oil, sprinkle with paprika and bake in a moderate oven (350°F.) for about thirty minutes until nicely brown.

(301) **Butter Bean Pie**

1½ cups dried butter beans,
pre-cooked
½ cup finely chopped onions
or leeks
½ cup finely chopped celery
¼ cup chopped peanuts
2 beaten eggs
½ cup water
sea salt or kelp to taste
1 cup mashed potato
1 tbs. (scant) oil

Preheat oven to 350°F.
Thoroughly mix the butter beans, onions, celery, nuts, eggs, water and sea salt in a bowl. Turn the mixture into an oiled pie dish and press down evenly. Cover with potato, smooth over with a knife and sprinkle with oil. Bake in a moderate oven (350° F.) for about forty minutes or until the surface is well browned.

(302) **Carrot and Chives Cutlets***

2 cups cooked potatoes
2 tbs. chopped chives
1 large carrot, finely grated
2 tbs. finely chopped peanuts
2 tbs. potato flour
½ tsp. sea salt or kelp
1 beaten egg
soya flour to coat
2 tbs. oil

Mash the potatoes with a fork until quite smooth. Mix in the chives, carrot, peanuts, potato flour and salt. Shape into cutlets and set aside on a plate to dry. Dip the cutlets in the egg and coat with soya flour. Heat the oil in a pan and fry the cutlets until lightly browned on both sides. Serve with a green leaf salad.

(303) **Carrot and Potato Flour Loaf**

2 cups grated raw carrot
1 cup grated celery
⅓ cup oil
1½ cups potato flour
4 tbs. soya flour
2 lightly beaten eggs
sea salt or kelp

Preheat oven to 325°F.

Mix the carrots, celery, oil and potato flour, then blend in the soya flour. Pour the beaten eggs over the mixture and stir well, adding salt or kelp to taste. Turn into an oiled casserole and bake at 325°F. for about one hour or until set. Serve with greens or a green leaf salad.

(304) **Carrot Savory Cakes**

2 raw egg yolks
4 tbs. oil
2 sieved hardboiled egg yolks
1 tsp. grated onion
2 cups grated carrot
½ tsp. sea salt

Preheat oven to 425°F.

Beat the raw egg yolks in a bowl. Set a little aside for dipping then add the heated oil and cook in a pan of boiling water until thickened. Mix in the rest of the ingredients, chill and shape into flat cakes. Dip in beaten egg. Bake at 425°F. until browned. Serve with emerald potatoes (285) and a green leaf vegetable.

(305) **Chestnut and Onion Pie (Baked)**

1 lb. chestnuts
6 medium onions
1 to 2 tbs. oil for frying
2 tbs. oil for mixing
mashed potato to thicken
pinch of sea salt

Preheat oven to 350°F.

Boil the chestnuts until tender—about twenty to thirty minutes and remove the skins. Peel and chop the onions finely and fry in the oil. Stir the mashed potato into some of the oil and pour this over the onions, stirring all the time, and adding the rest of the oil. Pour into a casserole add the chestnuts and mix together. Cover the casserole and cook in a moderate oven (350°F.) till thoroughly heated through. Serve with cooked greens or a green salad.

(306) **East Indian Curried Cabbage** (no curry powder)*

2 tbs. oil
2 tbs. chopped onion, shallots or apple
vegetable or plain water as required
3 cups chopped cabbage
½ tsp. turmeric
1 chili (optional)
1 tsp. chopped parsley
pinch of sea salt

Heat the oil in a pan, toss in the onion (or shallots or apple) and cabbage and cook until the onion is transparent only. Add enough water to moisten well and stir in the turmeric and chili if desired. Simmer gently for about three minutes longer. Remove while the cabbage is still crisp. Sprinkle with parsley and serve with any cold or hot dish, or on its own, surrounded by steamed potatoes.

(307) **Eggs Baked in Tomatoes**

4 medium tomatoes
4 eggs
2 tbs. oil
pinch of sea salt

Scoop out enough pulp from each tomato to leave room for an egg and set the pulp aside for addition to a gravy, soup or stew. Crack an egg into each tomato and sprinkle with salt. Set the tomatoes in an oiled baking dish or individual oven-proof dishes and bake until the egg is set. Serve with steamed potatoes and a white and red cabbage salad.

(308) **Lentil Flatties***

1 cup lentils
1 cup water
1 tbs. oil
1 chopped onion
1 pulped tomato
½ tsp. sea salt
pinch of thyme
2 tbs. mashed potato
1 beaten egg
2 tbs. oil for frying
paprika or soya flour

Wash the lentils, cover them with water and leave overnight. Next day place in a pan and add the onion, tomato, oil and seasoning. Cover the pan and simmer for two hours. Stir in the potato and continue to stir for about ten minutes until the mixture is stiff. Cool and form into flat cakes. Dip in beaten egg, shake in a paper bag with the paprika or soya flour and sauté in oil and brown on both sides. Serve with chopped chives.

(309) Lentil Roast*

1½ cups cooked lentils
1 cup mashed potatoes
½ cup dried beans, soaked overnight
½ cup chopped peanuts
½ cup water
1 to 2 tsp. sea salt
½ tsp. sage or thyme

Preheat oven to 350°F.
Mix the lentils and mashed potato in a bowl. Liquidize the soaked beans in a blender with their soaking water and add them to the bowl. Stir in the chopped nuts and the rest of the ingredients, mixing thoroughly. Bake in a covered oiled dish at 350° F. for twenty minutes, then cook them uncovered for ten minutes till nicely browned. Garnish with parsley.

(310) Baked Stuffed Mushrooms

8 fairly large mushrooms
2 tbs. oil
2 tbs. potato flour
½ pint soya milk
1 sprig each parsley and thyme, chopped
1 shallot or small onion, chopped
1 lightly beaten egg

Preheat oven to 450°F.
Remove the stalks and flesh of the mushrooms and sauté the outside cases and stalks in heated oil. Stir the potato flour into the soya milk, then add the mushroom flesh, parsley, thyme and shallot. Add and stir in the oil in which the cases were sautéed and the beaten egg. Stir over a gentle heat until the mixture thickens. Fill the mushroom cases with the mixture, stand a stalk on each and bake at 450°F. for five minutes. Serve on a hot dish garnished with parsley.

(311) Nut Savory (uncooked)

1 pulped tomato
4 oz. shredded coconut
4 oz. ground filberts
1 tsp. finely grated onion
mashed potato to stiffen
sea salt to taste
1 tsp. chopped marjoram or basil

Pour the tomato over the coconut shreds and leave to soak for a few minutes. Beat with a fork and add the rest of the ingredients, adding enough mashed potato to make a stiff mixture. Press the mixture into an oiled bowl, cover and chill. Serve sliced with jacket potatoes and a green salad The mixture keeps for one to three days.

(312) **Omelet (basic)**

4 to 6 eggs (at room temperature)
2 tbs. cold water
sea salt
1 tsp. oil

Beat the eggs long enough to mix the yolks and whites well, then add the water and sea salt to taste. Heat a pan and brush it with oil. Pour in the eggs and heat slowly for five to ten minutes, loosening the sides with a spatula and folding towards the center, letting any uncooked egg run to the sides. Cover the pan and heat slowly for another five minutes. Fold the edges to the center and sprinkle with chopped parsley, chives or paprika. Any diced cooked vegetable may be mixed with the eggs or folded in before the omelet is completely cooked.

(313) **Pea Cakes (Savory)***

1½ cups split peas, soaked overnight
½ cup water the peas were soaked in
½ tsp. sea salt
1 chopped onion
few sprigs of mint, chopped
1 cup dry mashed potato
paprika or soya flour

Preheat oven to 350°F.

Liquidize the peas, water and seasonings in a blender until very fine. Pour over the potato in a bowl and mix to a stiff dough, adding more potato as required. Shape into flat cakes and set aside on a large plate for half an hour to dry out. Sprinkle with paprika (or soya flour). Set out in an uncovered, oven-proof dish and bake at 350°F. for ten minutes. Turn and bake for ten minutes more.

(314) **Peanut and Potato Loaf***

3 cups mashed potatoes
1 onion, chopped and sautéed in oil
1 cup chopped celery or carrot
1 cup minced peanuts
grating of nutmeg
3 tbs. finely chopped parsley
1 beaten egg
1 tsp. sea salt or kelp

Preheat oven to 350°F.
Mix all ingredients thoroughly, adding a little water if the mixture is too dry, turn it into an oiled loaf tin and bake at 350°F. for thirty minutes.

(315) **Pease Pudding***

1 cup split peas
1 small onion
1 clove
1 tsp. sea salt
1 (scant) tbs. oil
1 egg
chopped chives

Preheat oven to 350°F.
Cover the peas with water and set aside for three hours, then simmer them with the onion, clove and salt until tender. Add the oil. Beat the egg and stir it into the mixture. Turn the mixture into an oiled oven-proof dish and bake for forty-five minutes at 350° F. Sprinkle with chopped chives and serve with potatoes and broccoli. (Broccoli provides three-quarters as much calcium as the same quantity of milk.)

(316) **Potato Flour Savory Pancakes**

1 tsp. sea salt
1 pint boiling water
5 oz. potato flour
cooked vegetable for stuffing

Add the salt to the water, then pour in the potato flour, stirring constantly and bringing back rapidly to a boil. Cook until thoroughly thickened, then remove the dough from the pan, pat it into rounds and cook in a heavy frying pan brushed with oil, or on a griddle. Turn the pancake when brown to brown the other side. Serve hot with any desired cooked vegetable rolled inside as stuffing. (Lentil or pea flour may be used instead of potato flour.)

(317) Potato Savories*

4 chilled, unpeeled potatoes
1 small onion
1 tsp. sea salt or kelp
1 lb. potato flour

Grate or finely shred the potatoes on to a paper towel and squeeze dry. Place them in a bowl, add the grated onion and salt and mix well, adding enough potato flour to make a stiff paste. Drop the paste by spoonfuls into hot oil in a pan and sauté until well browned on both sides. Serve with chopped parsley.

(318) Savory Beans*

2 tbs. oil
1 large onion, finely chopped
1 cup tomatoes, finely chopped
1 tsp. sea salt or kelp
1 tsp. dark molasses
2 cups cooked butter beans
2 tbs. chopped chives

Heat the oil in a pan and sauté the onions and tomatoes until tender. Add the sea salt, molasses and beans, cover and heat well. Serve garnished with chopped chives.

(319) Savory Steamed Eggs

3 eggs
¾ pint soya milk (73)
2 tbs. oil
1 tsp. sea salt
2 tbs. finely chopped chives or green part of spring onions or young leeks
paprika

Beat the eggs in a large bowl with a rotary beater. Add the other ingredients and beat well again. Pour into a deep casserole, cover and place in a steamer, or on a rack over boiling water in a saucepan, and cook steadily but not too vigorously for twenty minutes. Sprinkle with paprika and serve.

(320) Soya Bean Shepherd's Pie

2 cups vegetable stock or water
4 small onions
1½ cups chopped carrots
1½ cups cooked soya beans (drained)
½ cup soya flour
1 tsp. sea salt
1 tsp. dried marjoram
2 cups salted hot mashed potatoes
1 tbs. oil

Preheat oven to 350°F.

Heat the water or stock to boiling, add the onions and carrots, cover and cook until the carrots are tender. Add the soya beans, soya flour and seasoning, mix lightly and pour into a baking dish. Spread with the mashed potato, rough the surface with a fork and brush it with oil. Bake at 350°F. for about fifteen minutes, until the top is a golden brown.

(321) **Vegetable Casserole***

1 cup shredded raw potato
2 cups shredded raw carrot
1 cup finely sliced onions
2 tbs. soya flour
1 tsp. sea salt or kelp
½ tsp. honey
1 cup raw tomato juice (reserve the pulp for stews, etc.)

Preheat oven to 350°F.

Blend all ingredients thoroughly into a bowl to make a wettish mixture. Add a little more soya if too moist. Turn the mixture into an oiled casserole, cover tightly, and bake for about thirty minutes in a moderate oven (350°F.).

(322) **Vegetable Cutlets**

2 onions
2 carrots
1 potato
½ cup finely ground peanuts
½ cup soya flour
1 tsp. sea salt or kelp
2 well beaten eggs
2 tbs. oil
potato flour as required

Mince the onions, carrots and potato finely or shred them on a grater. Combine them with the ground peanuts, soya flour, salt and eggs. If the mixture is not dry enough add potato flour. Spread it out on a plate and chill for thirty minutes, then shape into cutlets. Heat the oil in a pan and fry the cutlets until they are well browned, turning to brown the second side, or brush with oil and broil until brown on both sides.

(323) **Vegetable Loaf (Steamed)**

2 tbs. oil
1 cup finely chopped tomatoes
1 cup finely chopped onions
¼ cup minced or finely chopped peanuts
2 beaten eggs
2 tbs. soya flour
2 tbs. split pea flour
¼ cup vegetable stock or water
grating of nutmeg
½ tsp. sea salt
½ tsp. basil or marjoram
1 tbs. minced parsley

Heat the oil and sauté the tomatoes and onions lightly. Blend with the rest of the ingredients and turn the mixture into an oiled pudding basin. Cover the basin tightly and steam for one-and-a-half hours. Set the pudding aside for ten minutes, then unmold. Chill and serve in slices. Or, the loaf may be kept in the basin, chilled and taken along on a picnic.

Suggested Reading

Crook, William G., M.D. *Are You Allergic? A Guide to Normal Living for Allergic Adults and Children*. Jackson, Tennessee: Professional Books, Box 3494, 1974.

Dickey, Lawrence D., M.D., ed. *Clinical Ecology*. Springfield, Illinois: Charles C. Thomas, 1976.

Golos, Natalie and Golbitz, Frances Golos. *Coping with Your Allergies*. New York: Simon and Schuster, 1979.

Ludeman, Kate, Ph.D. and Henderson, Louise. *Do-It-Yourself Allergy Analysis Handbook*. New Canaan, Connecticut: Keats Publishing, 1979.

Mackarness, Richard, M.D. *Eating Dangerously, the Hazards of Hidden Allergies*. New York: Harcourt Brace Jovanovich, 1976.

Mandell, Marshall, M.D., and Scanlon, Lynne Waller. *5-Day Allergy Relief System*. New York: Thomas Y. Crowell, 1979.

Philpott, William H., M.D. and Kalita, Dwight K., Ph.D. *Brain Allergies: The Psychonutrient Connection*. New Canaan, Connecticut: Keats Publishing, 1980.

Randolph, Theron G., M.D. *Human Ecology and Susceptibility to the Chemical Environment*. Springfield, Illinois: Charles C. Thomas, 1962.

Rowe, Albert H., M.D. and Rowe, Albert, Jr., M.D. *Food Allergy, Its Manifestations and Control, and the Elimination Diets*. Springfield, Illinois: Charles C. Thomas, 1972.

Sheinkin, David, M.D., Schachter, Michael, M.D. and Hutton, Richard. *The Food Connection: How the Things You Eat Affect the Way You Feel—And What You Can Do About It*. New York: Bobbs-Merrill, 1979.

INDEX

INDEX